REWILDING

THE WEST

REWILDING

THE WEST

RESTORATION IN A PRAIRIE LANDSCAPE

RICHARD MANNING

UNIVERSITY OF CALIFORNIA PRESS

BERKELEY   LOS ANGELES   LONDON

University of California Press, one of the most distinguished
university presses in the United States, enriches lives around the
world by advancing scholarship in the humanities, social sciences,
and natural sciences. Its activities are supported by the UC Press
Foundation and by philanthropic contributions from individuals
and institutions. For more information, visit www.ucpress.edu.

University of California Press
Berkeley and Los Angeles, California

University of California Press, Ltd.
London, England

Library of Congress Cataloging-in-Publication Data

Manning, Richard, 1951–.
   Rewilding the West : restoration in a prairie landscape /
Richard Manning.
       p.   cm.
   Includes bibliographical references and index.
   ISBN 978-0-520-25658-3 (cloth : alk. paper)
   1. Prairie restoration—Great Plains.   2. Great Plains—
History.   I. Title.
QH104.5.G73M36   2009
333.74′1530978—dc22   2008043137

Manufactured in the United States of America

18 17 16 15 14 13 12 11 10 09
10 9 8 7 6 5 4 3 2 1

This book is printed on Cascades Enviro 100, a 100% post
consumer waste, recycled, de-inked fiber. FSC recycled certified
and processed chlorine free. It is acid free, Ecologo certified,
and manufactured by BioGas energy.

CONTENTS

One

VISION

The most destructive force in the American West is its commanding views, because they foster the illusion that *we* command.

I am a westerner by choice, drawn to live here a quarter century ago by nothing so much as those views. The vistas are the antithesis of the claustrophobic forests of the upper Midwest, where I grew up. Like most newcomers, I was drawn first to the mountains, to the northern Rockies. The pristine peaks set in achingly blue sky and the vast wilderness areas stalked by cougars, wolves, and bears capture a man's imagination. Over the years, though, I found myself working down from the mountaintops toward the flat base. The eastern face of the Rockies, where the mountains abruptly and dramatically rise from the plains, is called "the Front Range."

I was drawn there by an illusion. It is the edge of the mountains, therefore the edge of wilderness, which is to say, of wildness. As I sit here facing east, everything behind me in the mountains is wild; everything in front is worked hard by farmers, cattle and sheep, oilmen, miners, and railroaders. Elevated a bit by wild mountains, the sweep of plains fosters the illusion that here, sheltered and informed by wilderness, one can see all of the rest, all of the space stretching east to the Mississippi, not just in three dimensions, but in four, in time, in its history.

Once you know a bit of this history, you can imagine easily enough that you see below great herds of bison, Chief Joseph fleeing, Custer's arrogance corrected, Jim Hill's railroaders pounding spikes and felling timber for ties, steam tractors gang-plowing wheatland, cattle drives, and even the great cloud of dust that rose from this land in the Dirty Thirties to create our nation's most profound environmental catastrophe, the scars of which remain.

Where else can one do this? I have sat on Appalachian and Adirondack mountainsides. But those vistas never allowed me to presume for a second that I knew a thing about conditions even a county away, so varied and inscrutable is the landscape. Yet again and again I have looked across the plains and believed I could literally see the conditions and history of everything east to the Mississippi, north to Alberta and Saskatchewan, south to Texas. I am a sucker for this illusion even now, when I understand how dangerous it is. The truth is, we do not know this landscape, not at all. Deceiving ourselves into believing we do is precisely why this land grows nothing so much as failure.

The northern Great Plains, no matter where they are viewed, are empty, becoming every year more vacant. People have made them what they are. Every single square inch of them is covered with evidence of human habitation and folly, and that's the point. To know a bit of this place's history is to know it is not an isolated, forgotten stretch of the human experience, "flyover country," as it is called by our nation's predominantly bicoastal population. The bedrock assumptions that shaped our nation played out and failed right here in the northern Great Plains. A harsh god of a landscape tested what we thought were our best ideas and found them wanting.

Obviously, the plains generated the western myth—the swaggering cowboy, the fast-gun vigilante, the boomer who is our entire nation's image worldwide today—but if you follow the human tracks far enough here, you quickly discover a forgotten story. True, this was the hallowed ground of Manifest Destiny, the ultimate frontier of a frontier people, but it was also shaped by Theodore Roosevelt and especially by his young cousin Franklin, a couple of knickerbockers. More important, it shaped them and their pivotal ideas. This is the foundation landscape of progressivism as it evolved under Theodore Roosevelt. The Great Plains are also the home soil of Franklin Roosevelt's New Deal and the social welfare state that persists, especially in the red-state West. This will be one of the cases I make in this book, that the progressive zeal of the reformer is every bit as dangerous as the swagger of the cowboy, and, conversely, the "conservative" West is almost wholly a creature of the nation's most socialist of projects, the New Deal. Cowboy myth and New Deal alike were flawed by the illusion of omniscience, an illusion encouraged by the wide-open spaces. Falling for this illusion is not without precedent.

The artist George Catlin made his way up the Missouri River in 1832 to Fort Union, an outpost at the confluence with the Yellowstone River in what is now Montana. He left us with fascinating drawings of Indian life but also letters describing the place. Among them is this:

> It is generally supposed and familiarly said, that a man "falls" into a reverie; but I seated myself in the shade a few minutes since, resolved to *force* [emphasis his] myself into one; and for this purpose I laid open a small pocket-map of North America, and excluding my thoughts from every other object in the world, I soon succeeded in producing the desired illusion. This little chart, over which I bent, was seen in all its parts as nothing but the green and vivid reality. I was lifted up upon an imaginary pair of wings, which easily raised and held me floating in the open air, from whence I could behold beneath me the Pacific and Atlantic Oceans—the great cities of the East, and the mighty rivers. I could see the blue chain of the great lakes at the North—the Rocky Mountains, and beneath them and near their base, the vast, and almost boundless plains of grass, which were speckled with bands of grazing buffaloes![1]

Catlin witnessed the beginning of the end of the bison. Although the actual fact of their near extermination would not be accomplished for another fifty years, he could see it coming even then. The hide trade was flourishing all around him, meaning bison were rapidly being converted into robes, then all the rage in upscale eastern carriages. His solution to this was interesting, in that his idea came a full forty years before the creation of the nation's first national parks at Yellowstone and Yosemite, an idea then regarded as original and America's gift to the world. Here's what he envisioned from his god's-eye view:

> And what a splendid contemplation too, when one (who has traveled these realms, and can duly appreciate them) imagines them as they *might* in the future be seen (by some protecting policy of government) preserved in their pristine beauty and wildness, in a *magnificent park*, where the world could see for ages to come, the native Indian in his classic attire, galloping his wild horse, with sinewy bow, and shield and lance, amid the fleeting herds of elk and buffaloes. What a thrilling specimen for America to preserve and hold up to the view of her refined citizens and the world in future ages! A *nation's Park*, containing man and beasts, in all the wild and freshness of their nature's beauty![2]

A painter is a seer, as is a photographer. L. A. Huffman was both photographer and bison hunter in Montana in the 1880s. Most of the bison were then gone, but after a night huddled against a prairie blizzard with his horse, Crackers, he wrote:

> When not busy melting snow in an army cup or toasting hard bread and bits of bacon over my tiny fire I talked to Crackers of my scheme to make a great pasture of the "Flat Iron" [the stretch of Montana between the Yellowstone and Missouri rivers, the very landscape that will be this book's focus], to fence it with a great woven wire to banish forever the skin hunters, maybe enlist them in an army of wardens. How and where the great park gates should be guarded, how tame wild things would get—bison, antelope and elk—and too, how splendid would be when the yellow-green carpet of spring had come, to see it all teeming with life.[3]

❧

Technology has computerized the process of being "lifted up upon an imaginary pair of wings." During the 1980s and '90s, computer software known as "geographic information systems" revolutionized the field of geography and our understanding of the state of nature. This technology does essentially what Catlin imagined he did with his pocket map. Using both aerial and satellite imagery as well as infrared photos that highlight aspects such as vegetative cover and topography, stream flow and seasonal changes, the computers draw maps that are used to organize and locate data such as wildlife populations, human populations, archaeological sites, and ownership boundaries. A computerized GIS overlays information on space. It allows one to ask sophisticated layers of questions about the land, at almost any scale, from an acre to a continent. You can sit at the computer screen and quickly generate the convincing illusion that you can see it all, from Rockies to Mississippi, even know it all.

It is a terribly saddening exercise. I've seen it applied to landscapes ranging from coastal rain forests to deserts, from city-plagued estuaries to logged-off mountain peaks. All of these maps are sober and unflinching accounts of our thorough mistreatment of the land. Yet the exercise is most stunning when applied to the vast sweep of grassland that is the center band of our continent, part of the globe's inventory of a biome known as temperate grasslands. (The other temperate grasslands occur largely across Eurasia in a belt below Siberia, in Australia, New Zealand, and the veldts of South Africa, and in South America in the pampas, which stretch east of the Andes through central Argentina.)

A scan of the North American stretch shows a negative, a record of absence. No passenger pigeons. No wild bison. Prairie dog colonies shrunk to the merest of dots. Black-footed ferrets down to, at the extreme, seven individuals. Swift foxes nearly gone. Same with prairie falcons and peregrines. Every watercourse dammed and drained.

Everything plowable plowed. That last circumstance is responsible for the extinctions. Temperate agriculture—by which we mean largely the production of corn, wheat, and beef—thrives only in temperate grasslands. That is why the above-mentioned inventory of the grasslands worldwide accounts for something like 90 percent of the world's agricultural exports.[4]

There is another absence to be recorded here, though: that of people. Cities aside, the population of the North American grassland peaked just after the end of World War I and has been in steady decline ever since. In contrast with that decline, the temperate grasslands, which are the world's breadbaskets, disproportionately bear the crushing burden of feeding the world's population. All other biomes—temperate and tropical rain forests, boreal forests, tundra, deserts, and such— are given some sort of protected status; that is, around 10 percent of their area is saved as parks and preserves in conditions that are close to the original, with wild native flora and fauna.[5] Temperate grasslands are a glaring exception. Only 1 percent of them is so protected. Agriculture gets what it wants.

Yet we are now learning that this least protected of landscapes was likely to have produced the most wildlife in former times. Creatures favored these places for the very reason agriculture does. Native grassland systems produce enormous amounts of that palatable commodity, grass, and because ungulates eat grass, the prairie can host a food chain with one very hefty link, a link capable of supporting bison and elk by the millions as well as the magnificent top-end predators, such as grizzly bears, which are the planet's most threatened category of wild animals. We know of this productivity from the reports of the people who encountered it and presided over its liquidation during the second half of the nineteenth century. Yet as we increasingly value wildlife and become more sophisticated in its protection, we realize that by maintaining a few remnant wildlife populations in Rocky Mountain parks and wilderness areas, we are swimming against a swift current. Elk, grizzlies, and wolves are plains animals, and we would get far greater results for our efforts by returning them to their habitat of choice.

❦

All of these facts slowly built a case, which in turn built a coalition of conservation groups in the American plains in the 1990s. The coalition included the usual suspects, such as Defenders of Wildlife, the Sierra Club, and the World Wildlife Fund, as well as local groups. The logical and chosen path for these conservationists was to enlist the support of the computers of Bill Haskins. I've known Haskins for almost twenty years, encountering him first when I was an environmental reporter for the local newspaper in Missoula, Montana. He was then a radical, allying himself with the town's active Earth First group. It's not clear whether his beliefs have mellowed over the years, but his tactics certainly have changed. He is an expert in GIS technology and has a rack of equipment that is the heart of a nonprofit advocacy group. Haskins's software has worked its way through the Great Plains, repeating Catlin's conceit using more concrete methods.

He and a group of biologists and ecologists from a number of conservation groups were looking for some stars to align. They asked questions of the landscape: Where were the largest chunks of undisturbed prairie? Where were the best habitat, the most endangered species, the biggest chunks of public land? And, especially, where was ranching in the worst financial trouble? The last question is key to their work. Formally, the mapping led to a research publication called *Ocean of Grass*, but this was no ordinary academic exercise.[6] It was an exercise in thinking big, simply because we have learned that conservation in this arid place must occur on an enormous scale.

The grassland has always been a landscape of motion. Its human inhabitants worldwide are largely nomads. Its big animals are migratory. Grasslands are grasslands because the aridity is further plagued by periodic droughts, as well as severe blizzards, wind, and a gauntlet of other brutal conditions. To survive all these, animals must be able to move to greener pastures, to protected coulees, to plateaus swept clean of snow by wind. All of this makes conservation of plains habitat and fauna a matter of large scale. A few hundred, even a few thousand, acres won't support wild bison, never mind the big predators that eat them. A viable plot for plains conservation is something on the order of four million acres.

The second element of the big thinking of Haskins and his colleagues involved a new idea in conservation that explains the economic questioning during their GIS mapping. As we shall see in detail as this story unwinds, the West is a welfare state built on public lands. A series of failed ideas and busted programs have left the landscape in a "checkerboard" condition. That is, square chunks of privately owned ranches are interspersed with even larger stretches of federal property, but the patchwork appears to be seamless in aerial views. That's because the federal land, virtually every square inch of it, is leased to those neighboring private ranches at well below market rates. Generally, the leases attach to the ranches as something very close to a property right, a matter that has been the chief vexation of western conservationists for generations.

The ranchers overgraze these federal lands, yet the laws give them almost complete freedom to do so, in the same way that a pre–Civil War plantation owner was free to beat and even kill his slaves. Someone, however, finally figured out that this vexation has presented an opportunity in disguise. If one were to become one of those ranchers, one would be as free to heal the land as the rancher historically was to abuse it. So what if we were to identify an area of, say, 3.5 million acres with a small amount of privately owned land and big chunks of federally leased grazing lands? And what if we were to buy all those private ranches? Conservationists would control the whole 3.5 million, to begin creating what Catlin called "a nation's park," what we will call "the American Prairie Reserve."

Map 1. The Great Plains. Courtesy of OnEarth *magazine.*

The *Ocean of Grass* study, with its god's-eye view, found ten spots in the American and Canadian plains that looked especially promising as testing grounds for this idea. One of those ten areas shone like a particularly bright beacon. This book is the story of that special place. The area called "the Northwest Glaciated Plains" is bounded on its south edge by the jagged line of the Missouri River. (See map 1.) This line describes a strip of glacier-and-flood-carved land that is generally known in eastern Montana as "the Missouri Breaks," where the flat plain "breaks" to form the river basin.

✍

One need not have GIS software to find the Missouri Breaks. A sense of the history of the general folly of the West will steer you toward this particular place at the heart of the plains and at the heart of this book. The most egregious examples of failed ideas keep cropping up around the Breaks. The tracks of both Roosevelts occur here, literally. In the end, it's as if the whole American enterprise, indeed the whole European enterprise, the notion of our relationship with the land, finally foundered on these very western rocks—and this is one of the cases I will explore in this book—so much so that any attempt to undo the damage, any attempt to rewrite western civilization's founding story, must begin in Phillips County, Montana.

But find the Missouri Breaks first on map 2, zero in on it, just as Haskins's computer did, and understand the promise of this place. Begin at its epicenter in a mostly forgotten but rare bit of wildlife habitat, a million acres that is the Charles M. Russell National Wildlife Refuge, its very existence a happy accident of history. Add to that a strip of mostly federal land that has already been designated as the Upper Missouri Breaks National Monument. Now draw a big, vague, wobbly sort of concentric circle—an oval really—around this core of federal land, a circle that encompasses an additional 2.5 million acres, for a total of about 3.5 million acres. This is the area proposed as the American Prairie Reserve. Notice that the Missouri River bisects this circle. If

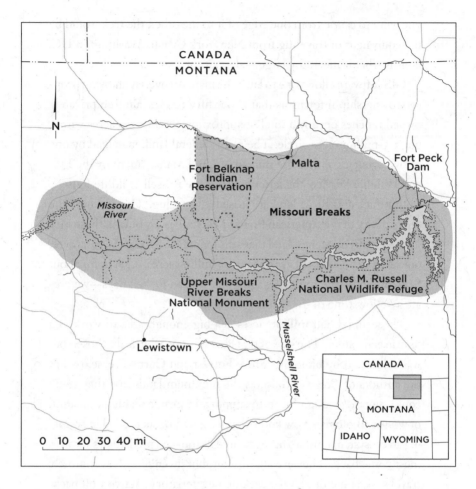

Map 2. The area of the proposed American Prairie Reserve (indicated by shading).
Courtesy of Northern Plains Conservation network.

one were to canoe from one edge of it to the other, the trek would be the equivalent of traveling from New York City to Washington DC. This is what is meant by large scale.

GIS software allows one to layer the map. An overlay showing property ownership informs us that about fifty to one hundred privately owned ranches occupy a total of approximately 800,000 acres within our 3.5-million-acre circle. The rest is federal land, managed by one of two agencies, either the Bureau of Land Management or the Fish and Wildlife Service; the latter controls the Russell Wildlife Refuge. Both refuge and BLM land are leased for grazing. This is where the opportunity of the American Prairie Reserve lies. By buying those fifty to one hundred ranches, land that sells for maybe $200 or $300 an acre, one leverages control of grazing on 3.5 million acres. That is, for about $250 million—the price of waging war in Iraq for ten days—we create a Yellowstone of the plains.

Three and a half million acres is a big enough area to work as a prairie ecosystem. The size of that area was not arbitrarily chosen but was calculated by biologists Steve Forrest and Curtis Freese, two of the authors of *Ocean of Grass*, as the minimum landscape they think could support enough bison to support, in turn, a viable population of wolves. Biologists now know that we have not succeeded in restoring an ecosystem until we have restored its top-end predators, so wolves must come back. They are absent now, but juvenile wolves routinely travel several hundred miles seeking new territory. Active wolf packs are already that close to the Breaks, so restoring the habitat would bring them home, and this landscape is indeed restorable. Most of its native vegetation remains; the mapping has told us so. It is abused, but simply removing the cows could bring it back to life and would eventually allow the introduction of bison herds big enough to thunder. In fact, the first wild bison already occupy the first purchased ranch as I write this in 2008.

This is a grand idea worth pursuing, especially worth pursuing because it is so wound up in the larger American story. This is not a story of just conservation; it is the story of all of us.

For a couple of years now I have visited this landscape often. I leave my mountain home in western Montana and drive the six or seven hours to enter the Missouri Breaks by way of a fifty-five-mile-long gravel road straight south out of the closest town of any consequence, Malta, with a population of twenty-one hundred and falling. I often stop atop what passes for a hill in the short-grass prairie, a tawny landscape of gentle rolls like a cougar's hide. *Gentle*, however, is a seldom-used word in central Montana, a place of 50-below blizzards, 106-degree heat waves, and just enough annual rainfall to keep it from desiccating—at least officially—into desert.

From this hill, one can pan a full 360 degrees of almost straight, unbroken horizon line, treeless and vast as a sea. The only exceptions are the Little Rockies, seen to the northwest, forty to fifty miles away, and the Larb Hills, also forty to fifty miles away but in the opposite direction. Both features are within the project area. Pick the vantage right and the whole sweep will contain not a single building, no structure more significant than a rusting run of three-strand barbed-wire fence strung on steel posts. It's all grass—in the spring of a rare wet year, green native bunch grasses and sagebrush; by fall, grassland grazed hard and flat as a parking lot. "Cow-burned" is the apt and usual description.

This emptiness says "isolation," a misanthrope's paradise that keeps pulling me back, but the sense of emptiness is an illusion, part of the series of illusions this place generates. This, I have come to understand, is a human-formed landscape, an artifact of agriculture, and agriculture, through six thousand years, has evolved into the most environmentally destructive force on the planet. Fitting, then, that this little corner of the globe should now become a center of our struggle to counter that force.

The place may look empty, but it is haunted by a full population of ghosts. It is haunted by the American story, and a landscape that possesses a history so full and so relevant but is now so vacant is a wonder.

It strikes one at first as bleak, but this too is illusion. Properly understood, it is a landscape of promise and hope.

Two

ABORIGINAL SINS

The red man will be driven out and the white man will take possession.
This is not justice, but it is destiny.
— New York Times *editorial, April 15, 1875*

Prince Maximilian of Wied-Neuwied, a curious German nobleman, rode a steamboat up the Missouri River through the heart of the Breaks in 1833, bringing with him the artist Karl Bodmer, in the same way a tourist today would lug a camera. Only two years behind George Catlin, they made it more than three hundred miles farther upriver, to what is now the town of Fort Benton. Bodmer made the now-famous series of paintings intended as an accurate record of Indian life along the Upper Missouri, but it is from one of Maximilian's observations of a Piegan chief that an even more intricate picture emerges.[1] He noted meeting a chief called Iron Shirt, so named because he wore Spanish chain mail, probably from the American Southwest, a thousand miles away; such was the trade network of the day.

A more modern detail expands on Maximilian's observation: In the 1990s archaeologists found an ornate shell mask in the Sweet Grass Hills, about eighty miles north of Fort Benton, also within the territory of the Piegans, Bloods, and Siksikas—collectively, the Blackfeet. It was then about five hundred years old and made from seashells from the south Atlantic coast.[2] The western historian Richard White says,

"American Indian peoples have long been bemused at the idea that Europeans not only discovered their land but also somehow discovered them. And Indian peoples are right to find European pretensions somewhat silly. The exploration of the West has meaning only in terms of European ignorance, not in terms of any contribution to universal knowledge."[3]

I began writing this during a year when Montana was awash in tourists marking the bicentennial of the Corps of Discovery, Lewis and Clark's explorations in 1805–6. Those idolizing the near illiterate explorers forget that their biggest discovery was America's own ignorance. But then Walter Prescott Webb, the great historian of the Great Plains, is even more dismissive of the venture: "Why a man of Jefferson's philosophical and scientific turn of mind should have been unable to select more capable men for the enterprise, keen observers with trained minds, is hard to understand."[4] I'm with Webb. Chain mail and shell masks tell us Lewis and Clark "discovered" primitive savages who had been engaged in cross-continent trade for centuries. The trail of discovery of these explorers was already well worn.

Yet today there is something that needs discovering, something we must know about ourselves in relation to early plains history, and it is, once more, our own ignorance. Exploring our ignorance of these matters involves not an academic but a biological question, which can lead to an economic answer. Biology has assembled some important ideas about what makes a given ecosystem endure. Why does the ecosystem of the Great Plains hold up over the long haul, especially given the poor soils and harsh climate? Part of that answer has to do with coevolved species, a given collection of plants and animals that evolution has fine-tuned not just to exist in a place but to exist, in fact to thrive, in and only in the presence of one another. This becomes a matter of economy when we realize grasslands are the most productive of systems in terms of biomass, plant mass that gets passed up the food chain. We are finally learning—and this story will be nothing so much as a summary of that hard learning—that every single thing

we neo-Europeans have done on the plains has compromised that productivity. The plains were not just biologically but also, by extension,
economically better off before we arrived.

Yet, if we are to learn to reassemble some of this productivity, we
must know something of the landscape's original condition, the relationships among all of its species, including humans. This is how we
must address sustainability. What sort of human endeavors will leave
this ecosystem intact and perpetual, as we assume it was when Maximilian and Catlin made their trips upriver and were struck by a land
awash in wildlife and big hunks of protein, which is to say productive?

The biologist's simple question about the period is this: What were
presettlement conditions, meaning what was it like before white settlers came? But this turns out to be the wrong question. Whites and
their commercial partners, the Indians, radically reshaped this land long
before Meriwether Lewis and William Clark were schoolboys skip-
ping spelling classes. That chain mail shirt came through trade, and
trade was indeed the motor force of this presettlement society. It was
a consumer and commercial society.

Popular imagination populates the presettlement plains with dances-
with-wolves Indians, idyllic tipi-dwelling nomads living off bison.
Indeed, this version of Indian history has been broadly generalized to
all North American tribes. Popular imagination makes tipis the universal aboriginal dwelling, but they were largely limited to the plains;
stereotypical mascot Indians of sports teams have full eagle-feather
headdresses, another plains affectation.

This misunderstanding is the result of more than just the silliness
of popular iconography. The plains tribes survived into the age of pho-
tography and recent memory, so our image of them is the clearest. The
nomadic plains tribes were the last of the North American natives to
be wiped out, largely because they were nomadic.

The hunters and gatherers and agricultural tribes east of the Mississippi, in the Southwest, and along the Pacific coast all encountered whites earlier than the plains tribes did, because they were sedentary. The better soils and other conditions allowed farming, and the better resources, such as fisheries and forests, allowed a more stable existence. But these circumstances also attracted the early attentions of the European settlers, who were farmers and wanted the same land. The northern plains were the last to be conquered, simply because they presented the most challenging landscape for European agriculture.

Hidden in this scenario is a subtler reason, though probably every bit as important, if not more so, for the endurance of the nomadic Indians. Diseases of European origin, especially smallpox, killed far more Indians than did genocidal warfare, simply because native peoples had no immunities to them. Dense, sedentary settlements are sitting ducks for communicable diseases, but nomadic hunters can better avoid contagion. There is some evidence the natives understood this.

For instance, the environmental historian Andrew Isenberg cites a Kiowa folk tale in which that tribe's trickster figure, Saynday, meets smallpox on the plains and suggests to the disease that it would be better off attacking the Kiowa's enemies, the Pawnees, who live in large settlements along rivers. Writes Isenberg, "Eurasian disease did not indiscriminately destroy all Indians. In the eighteenth century, epidemics flowed through the Great Plains like the waters of the Missouri River during a spring flood, inundating the (more densely settled) valleys but leaving the high ground unaffected."[5] As a result of all of this, many semiagricultural tribes abandoned their villages during that century because they had become too decimated by disease to be viable and too pressured by white settlers to be tenable. The former farmers became nomads.

Settlement and disease pushed this process of transformation, but horses pulled it. The ponies the Spanish had brought into the Southwest in the early seventeenth century had become the stock in trade of nomadic tribes by the end of that century. The Indians were drawn to the horses for the same reasons that European power in that era was based on the possession of horses. Mounted men could defeat the unmounted, precisely why European nobility has traced directly to equestrianism. In the plains, though, the horse gave the extra advantage of making it easier to hunt bison and to transport villages in order to follow the bison herds. Before, tribes had killed bison by organizing whole villages in drives to stampede herds off cliffs—bison jumps. In those days, dogs had effected transport.

∾

Wandering the Missouri Breaks and plains, one is struck first and always by the emptiness, by which I mean their emptiness of people. A quick read of the place's history says this is an illusion, that it teems with a human story, but a deeper read counters this. The answer as to what sort of human culture endures here is probably no sort at all. It has always been a place where people have come and gone.

Archaeology tells us humans have been here for at least ten thousand years. The Missouri River was the line of demarcation when humans first arrived, when the great ice sheet still spread south to form that river's bed. The river marked the ice sheet's southern, leading edge. The earliest native cultures hunted creatures such as mastodons in this very landscape, but we know almost nothing of the way they lived, other than that they were hunters. They spread throughout North and South America in a very short time. Signs of long-term human habitation on the plains, however, are few in contrast to those in most other areas of North America.

West of the plains in the moister and more temperate Rocky Mountains, such evidence exists. Splinters from tribes of the Pacific Northwest, largely Shoshonis, Flatheads, and Bannocks, migrated and settled there long ago, and they—not what we now regard as plains tribes—were probably the people who most used the plains, traveling there in annual summer migrations to hunt buffalo but heading back west to what we moderns call Montana's "banana belt" to sit out the winter. The western edge of the Rockies is really a part of the Pacific

Northwest, blessed by warm air off the ocean; the eastern side gets its winters from the Arctic Circle. To this day, no sane western Montanan would winter in the east if he could avoid it. The trail that Lewis and Clark followed into the Rockies was, by the time of their arrival, well used and marked with stone cairns. Some of those cairns still exist. The western tribes called the trail "cokhalarishkit," which translates as something like "going to get the bison."

The tribes that Lewis and Clark met on the plains were present largely as a result of the preceding centuries of European invasion. Just before 1800, the ferocious and archetypal Montana tribe the Blackfeet had moved into the northern plains from the northeast, in what is now central Canada. They drove the Shoshonis and Bannocks from their traditional hunting grounds. Of the three subsets of Blackfeet, the Piegans were the only ones to move into what is now Montana; the other two have remained in Alberta.

The Crows also migrated south out of central Canada, lived for a while in what is now North Dakota, then resumed a southwestern migration into what is now southern Montana around 1600. By 1800, they were firmly established there as horse-borne nomads. The Atsinas came from what is now Minnesota. The Assiniboine, closely related to the Sioux, came from the Mississippi headwaters. The Sioux themselves, the Dakota nation, were among the last to arrive, pushed out of the Great Lakes region and the Upper Mississippi woodlands and ever westward, beginning in the mid-seventeenth century, until they controlled most of the northern plains by the mid-nineteenth century. The northern Cheyenne moved into an area just south of the Sioux at about the same time.[6]

Late in the nineteenth century, the Chippewas and Crees, tribes associated with the upper Great Lakes, began filtering into the plains. Then, as if to signal the transition to come, the Metis arrived. Fiddle players, drivers of high-wheeled carts, the Metis were of a hybrid culture, drawn from long-established pairings of French Canadians and upper Great Lakes tribes. In the writings of early explorers, they are never identified as Metis, but simply as "breeds," a truncation of *half-breeds*, even so identified by one of Montana's earliest cattlemen, Granville Stuart, who himself was married to an Indian.

This, then, is the culture or mix of cultures that existed when the first whites arrived, the condition of presettlement. Was it sustainable? In one sense, hard to know, because it had not been sustained. Still, we can be tempted to say it was, because of those bounteous descriptions of a landscape teeming with wildlife. Yet this quick assessment ignores a common thread of each of these cultures: that they were in the plains to do business and were in fact deeply integrated in the global European economy, even when Lewis and Clark arrived. In the early nineteenth century, the business of the plains was the fur trade. The tales of abundance were also an illusion.

Wrapped up in the question of sustainability is another question, which serves as a portal to the larger one. Part of asking whether life is sustainable is asking whether life is good, whether it sustains human well-being. As we, the well fed, think of this, it is a question of values and cannot really be answered without placing ourselves in the mindset of, say, an Assiniboine Sioux. This, through history and across the globe, has proven an impossible exercise for civilized (by which I mean agricultural) people. Agricultural existence in its very essence means trading a certain amount of freedom for security; in exchange for a reliable stock of food, one is bound to the land and all of the stoop labor this implies, just as more generally one is bound to a lord, a priest, a tyrant, or a desk job for a kind of security. Through time, hunter-gatherers have lived in conditions we would regard as brutal, yet the curious matter here is that history mostly lacks examples of hunter-gatherers who, on seeing the conditions of civilized life, have willingly abandoned their brutal existence for it. But history possesses abundant examples of nomads who have died fighting rather than adopt the blessings of civilization.

This process of suppressing nomads is as old as civilization but is now mostly complete. Imperialism stoked the battle to such a full roar during the nineteenth century that it could be defined as conquering native hunter-gatherers. Both Europe and the United States produced a strong reaction to this conquering in the form of romantics, privileged people who idealized the noble savage. Catlin was among them, so one needs to try to see through the romantic filter that colors his description of the aboriginals of Montana Territory in 1832:

> The several tribes of Indians inhabiting the regions of the Upper Missouri, and of whom I spoke in my last Letter, are undoubtedly the finest looking, best equipped, and most beautifully costumed of any Continent. They live in a country well-stocked with buffaloes and wild horses, which furnish them an excellent and easy living; their atmosphere is pure, which produces good health and long life; and they are the most independent and the happiest races of Indians I have met with; they are all entirely in a state of primitive wildness, and consequently are picturesque and handsome, almost beyond description. Nothing in the world, of its kind, can possibly surpass in beauty and grace.[7]

Catlin is not alone in this view, then or now. In 1968, Marshall Sahlins called these people the "original affluent societies," an example Isenberg raises only to argue it. Says Isenberg, "His [Sahlins's] polemical attack on the assumption that hunter-gatherers lived a meager existence on the edge of starvation was a needed corrective to the prevailing notion that agriculture and sedentariness were necessarily more enlightened resource strategies than hunting and gathering. His generalizations are accurate for societies that relied primarily on gathering, but he minimized the inherent precariousness of societies that relied primarily on mammal hunting for their subsistence."[8]

Yet the plains dictate a life of mammal hunting simply because there are few edible plants to gather. The place's primary product is grass, and humans need ungulates to convert grass to protein and carbohydrates. Evolution has not equipped us with the teeth and digestive juices to do it ourselves. Droughts, severe winters, and migration of game ensure that lean times will occur on the plains, time of human hunger. The histories of the tribes themselves tell of starvation. So what was life like for these people—affluent or precarious?

We have ways of seeing beyond the subjective generalizations to the measurable. For instance, Catlin was struck by the stature of plains tribes. To the point of monotony, he reports on natives standing taller than six feet. That and the handsomeness he describes are measures of enduring well-being. Although it's true that genes provide the potential for one to be tall and good-looking, and possibly the natives were genetically so inclined, nutrition is necessary to reach that potential. The connection between nutrition and attractiveness is not as clear, but beauty, because it can be marred by scars from disease and asymmetries that accrue from poor nutrition in childhood, is a biological sign of fitness, an advertisement that one lives well. It is a display that attracts mates.

Our stereotype, for instance, says that South Asians are short people, yet as a middle class has developed in India, this has been disproven. In rural India, one is indeed surrounded by short people, but when standing at a cocktail party in a business-class hotel in Bangalore, one encounters stature similar to that found in Europe and the United States. Indeed, nineteenth-century Europeans would have commented on Native Americans as a race of tall people if only because people taller than six feet were an exceedingly rare sight in Europe at the time. The masses of Europe were undernourished and short. The Europeans who migrated to the New World were the exception that proved the rule. The colonies, with their sparse population, almost immediately yielded a bounty of food that within a generation made the colonists notably taller than their ancestors. In fact, that is one of the standout differences in skeletal remains of agricultural people compared with hunter-gatherers throughout the millennia. Almost universally, the hunter-gatherers are taller.

Catlin's observations on stature provide quantifiable evidence to back up his more romantic generalizations. Nonetheless, he was observing a society in flux and well may have encountered these prosperous aboriginals at the pinnacle of their success. They were living off abundance, but that abundance was transitory. Their congregation in what is now eastern Montana probably marks the first time this barren stretch had been permanently occupied by humans to any significant degree. They did not withdraw to western Montana in winters. Furthermore, environmental historians have argued that the abundance of bison and other ungulates in the region was the result of several factors. First, disease, especially smallpox, had so decimated human populations in the region, and had done so for generations, that the hunting pressure on big ungulates was greatly reduced. They thrived, as did their predators, such as grizzlies and wolves.

Second, the conquest of new territory when tribes pushed west created a sort of permanent warfare, battles over hunting territory, which also reduced the number of hunters. Catlin himself reported finding, on average, two women for every man in Indian villages, a phenomenon he attributes to death from warfare and hunting accidents. That same warfare, however, produced buffer zones, no-man's lands, particularly notable in areas near the feared Blackfeet. Those no-ride zones were game havens, and Caucasian explorers undoubtedly crossed into them without knowing what had created the abundance they observed.

Beyond these circumstances, though, was a set of principles that enabled this improvised and experimental plains economy. The founding facts of life of the presettlement plains pointed unmistakably to *un*sustainability, and Catlin knew it. These were the forces that provoked his dire warnings of the bison's extermination, which summarized his visit. Dress and beadwork aside, the Indians of the northern plains were at bottom engaged in an economy that was fundamentally unsustainable for two reasons: their dependence on horses and their trade in hides.

᧥

Some might call the horse the SUV of the presettlement plains, but that would trivialize its role. It was not some frill that the elite procured for their entertainment. Nor was its critical role a phenomenon limited to the plains. Horsepower was the power of the world and had been for thousands of years. Simple inventions such as the horse collar in China, about fifteen hundred years earlier, had brought a global agricultural revolution and population explosion.[9] Later, riders became knights and lords. Brought to the New World, horses proliferated by the thousands, even millions, to the marvel of Europeans. At one point, horses were so plentiful that Atlantic seaboard colonists simply went to the wilder places and captured what they needed. Horses were also newcomers to and proliferated wildly in the South American pampas, New Zealand, and Australia. They were an essential part of the virgin-soil phenomenon that gave these colonies—all in temperate grasslands, all colonized by Europeans, wheat, and cattle—their leg up on the rest of the world. Horses spread like weeds, which became a material point in the grasslands ecosystem.[10]

Weed is an ambiguous word. It can mean what it means to most people: a specially adapted plant that colonizes disturbed soil; a plant pest in fields and gardens. But the more consequential meaning is "an exotic." An exotic plant or animal or microbe is alien to a given ecosystem, something introduced, almost always by peripatetic humans. Without locally evolved controls such as predators, diseases, and competitors, some of these exotics proliferate, seemingly at the expense of everything else. In the end, exotics more than development and exploitation will take down our remaining intact ecosystems.

This is just why horses spread in the grassland colonies: they were exotics, a curious case in North America. In deep time, horses are more native to North America than almost any other surviving mammal. They evolved on the plains of the continent but went extinct along with mastodons and saber-toothed tigers. The surviving horses have descended from those that migrated across the Bering land bridge first to Eurasia, to revolutionize the Old World, and then eventually back again. Once back in the New, they fit as if evolved for the place, which they were, but they were still weeds in the sense that evolution had by then changed the rules of the game. The predators that had kept them in check millennia before were now extinct. More important, though, horses were vital to human society, both new European and native, so they became ubiquitous. Their comparison to SUVs is not as frivolous as it would seem at first; they, too, were hell on resources, but on an even greater scale than the SUV, almost on the scale of internal combustion. Damage from horses was particularly pronounced in the case of nomadic hunters, who were, first, almost wholly dependent on horses and, second, inhabitants of a brittle environment based in grass.

In the early nineteenth century, plains tribes maintained horse herds averaging from six to as many as fifteen horses per person. This means that a roving band of two hundred people would include a retinue of several thousand horses, enough to overgraze any area they occupied for any length of time and enough to damage streams where people camped and watered. The estimated native population at the time would have possessed as many as nine hundred thousand domestic horses. Another two million ran wild on the plains. Isenberg estimates that the 80 percent overlap between horse and bison diets was sufficient to displace as many as 2.3 million bison. The horse began rearranging the plains ecology.[11]

And it certainly rearranged plains society. Ordinarily, one acquires new horses through reproduction, but maintaining brood mares and feeding colts to maturity place an extra burden on resources. Stealing new horses was by far more efficient, and plains life demanded fundamental efficiency. Surviving lore and accounts of the day testify that this indeed was a basic activity of each of the plains tribes. Horse theft was a matter of pride, a way of humiliating one's enemies. Successful thieves were accorded positions of honor, as their role in the economy might imply. In part, this thievery was responsible for the more or less constant state of warfare that obtained among plains tribes.

All of this might have been sustainable if unaccompanied by other circumstances. In the fundamental economy, stealing horses was simply a way of redistributing wealth. Further, the ecosystem might have survived with the bison herds, estimated at about 30 million, losing forage for only 2.3 million of their numbers. In addition to participating in a society of theft, though, these natives were consumers. Our early observers were clear on this.

Prince Maximilian, although drawn to the plains by an Old World romantic image of the noble savage, describes a culture dominated by commerce. His time at Fort McKenzie—just upstream from the Missouri Breaks—is full of details of how that commerce worked with the Blackfeet and Gros Ventres and occasionally the Salish from across the Rockies. The whites, agents of the American Fur Company, offered firearms, knives, utensils, European-style clothing, blankets, paint, glass beads, and jewelry in trade for processed hides—wolf, beaver, and especially bison. The prince's account indicates the trade was pervasive and had thoroughly integrated the tribes in a commercial system. He describes his first encounter with a trading party of Blackfeet at Fort McKenzie: "The whole region was filled with groups of brown and brownish-red—the hides covering them are painted yellowish-red or reddish-brown—mass of humanity, who, some on foot, some on horseback, some spread in groups, along the bank, awaited us. Closely surrounding the fort were the men, about 806 Piegans or Piekuni, in a densely packed multitude, drawn up like a well-ordered battalion."[12]

The chiefs among these people were especially resplendent in European dress, including military uniforms, which were a primary trade good. But of more importance still was the whiskey, which, more than lubricating the trade, was in fact the basis of it. Maximilian reported that the whites were offering watered-down kegs of whiskey in "indescribable scenes" of "barter and bacchanalia." All told, the conversion of whiskey to hides realized the traders a profit of about 3,000 percent, Maximilian calculates.

Maximilian's and Catlin's reports trace a rapid transition on the plains. Catlin, only two years before Maximilian's trip, had been unable to make it beyond Fort Union, three hundred miles to the east of Fort McKenzie. According to his reports, Blackfeet were at Fort Union but by and large stubbornly resisted trade with the whites. By the time of Maximilian's visit, though, they had been seduced by trade goods and whiskey, the end of a process that had begun only thirty years before.

Maximilian and Catlin do agree on one element, that the trading sessions at both forts were multicultural events, including a wide variety of the tribes appearing to do business under an uneasy truce. Away from the forts, these tribes were bitter enemies, fighting largely over rights to hunting grounds, that is, over access to the raw material that fed the economy. It was a violent place, but most of the violence was not directed against whites. It was intertribal.

A couple of environmental historians have examined the detail of this economy with an eye toward its unsustainability. Dan Flores cites a number of factors pointing toward the bison's demise, including overuse by the native population, even without trade factored in.[13] The effects of their hunting were magnified by their preference for young females, which provided better meat and thinner, more luxurious robes, resulting in a huge hole in the reproductive population. This sort of hunting stressed the bison numbers to the point that they were less able to recover from periodic droughts, disease, and predation from wolves and grizzlies. But whatever the effects of subsistence hunting, the effects of the fur trade were far worse. Flores says Cheyenne on the southern plains were, by the 1850s, killing about twice as many bison as they needed for subsistence in order to feed the robe trade. Writes Isenberg, "With the onset of the robe trade, the plains nomads, like the Paleo-Indians who helped to destroy the large herbivores of the Pleistocene epoch, turned to the destruction of the bison."[14]

Catlin provides a scene that verifies the calculations:

The snow in these regions often lies during the winter to the depth of three or four feet, being blown away from the tops and sides of the hills in many places, which are left bare for the buffaloes to graze upon, whilst it is drifted in the hollows and ravines to a very great depth, and rendered almost entirely impassable to these huge animals, which, when closely pursued by their enemies, endeavour to plunge through it, but are soon wedged in and almost unable to move, where they fall an easy prey to the Indian, who runs up lightly upon his snow shoes and drives his lance to their hearts. The skins are then stripped off, to be sold to the Fur Traders, and the carcasses left to be devoured by the wolves. This is the season in which the greatest numbers of these animals are destroyed for their robes—they are most easily killed at this time, and their hair or fur being longer and more abundant, gives greater value to the robe.[15]

The term *robe* leads us to another fundamental element of this economy. The Indians were not trading in raw hides; the commercial tanning process for converting rawhide to leather would not come until the 1870s. Theirs was a finished product requiring a labor-intensive system that involved drying and softening the skin with the dense bison fur left in place. The robes were popular among civilized folks as carriage blankets. The same dense hair that uniquely equipped the bison to survive northern plains winters made such a blanket warmer than anything else. It was specifically Indian women who processed the green hides into finished products, which limited sales in proportion to the number of available women. At the same time, though, this convention added another layer of commerce in capital goods—trade in women.

Catlin offhandedly remarks, "Every one of these red sons of the forest (or rather of the prairie) is a knight and a lord—his squaws are his slaves."[16] That he does so in judging their life idyllic is a measure of the attitudes of the time; he doesn't relate the opinions of the women.

Nonetheless, we do know that Indian women were the targets of intertribal raids, just as horses were, and for similar reasons. A hunter's income was limited by how many wives he could keep. The two-to-one ratio of women to men provided some help in this, but also that ratio was probably influenced by the warfare over women.

The presence of male white traders exacerbated this pressure. Prince Maximilian reports that one trader paid one hundred dollars for his Indian bride (to be abandoned when he returned to the East), but the bride's family offered a horse and rifle to the trader as part of the bargain. It was to that family's advantage to maintain a close tie to the trader.

I don't raise these issues to criticize native society, to revise the standing revisionist history. Recall that, at bottom, this plains culture was not native but a creation of European intervention. Left to their own devices, the aboriginals would not have been there but would have remained in the more stable and fertile valleys they had long inhabited. It was, in many ways, an experimental culture, and some experiments need time to work. Given time and some stability, a system conscious of limits could have evolved, and it could have been more or less sustainable.

We now know what lay ahead for the plains: a future not of hunting and gathering but of agriculture. Given the long arc of history and the choices population pressure has imposed, it seems academic, even naive, to speculate on a future of hunting and gathering in this place. Nonetheless, this very speculation will guide my arguments as we begin to look squarely at how agriculture has operated in the bit of the northern plains that is our focus. For the moment, though, suffice it to say that modern ecologists have looked broadly and deeply at humanity's footprints on the planet and concluded that agriculture is by far our most destructive activity, because agriculture is fundamentally unsustainable. Further, hunting and gathering is not a relic. Humans now derive maybe 25 percent of their total sustenance from hunting and gathering, measured by tons of biomass, a figure that seems high until one realizes activities such as commercial fishing and logging do indeed qualify as hunting and gathering.

It may seem folly to argue that logging and fishing can be fundamentally sustainable, given the current crises of forests and oceans as a result of humanity's pillaging of those resources. Both of these matters, however, represent failures of regulation, just as did the near extinction of the bison during the nineteenth century. Almost any competent scientist could develop a system of rules and a schedule of harvest that would make either logging or commercial fishing sustainable. No scientist could develop such a system for agriculture. It is, at its roots (literally), unsustainable, for reasons we will explore later.

Could plains Indians have developed these regulations for bison hunting, given time? To some degree, they did. Some groups of Sioux, for instance, maintained a system of hunting marshals that regulated numbers killed and seasons of bison hunting, but those regulations tended to work best when the tribes were isolated. When tribes began competing for those same bison, a tragedy of the commons ensued. Further, superstition worked against the sort of rational evaluation of feedback loops that successful regulation requires. Most of the tribes believed that a spirit of the earth provided bison in abundance, and no matter how many were killed, the spirit would renew the resource, a belief that finds its parallel in the superstitions of modern, free-market, cornucopian economists and fundamentalist Christians.

More important, though, I think, is that any rational solution would have a hard time emerging from a market based on alcohol, as this one clearly was. We need only consider how the drug economy of modern cities and even small towns rests squarely on wanton theft—junkies stealing to support habits—to understand the problem. Native Americans, like most hunting peoples worldwide, share a genetic predisposition to alcoholism for exactly the same reason they have a predisposition to diabetes. They have not evolved the mechanisms for digesting alcohol and sugars as long-settled agricultural cultures have. Alcoholism remains the gravest problem of today's Indian people, the descendants of the very people Catlin and Maximilian met along the Missouri. The bison were, to borrow a psychobabbler term, the "enablers."

Still, other societies, left to their own devices, have come to grips with these problems. The history of protecting nature is not a corollary of the law of entropy. The hunting of the late nineteenth century brought deer, elk, and antelope to near extinction, along with the bison. None of those is in any way threatened with extinction today. We—or, more to the point, our regulations—have brought them back.

These experimental cultures of the northern plains, however, were not to be left to their own devices. The second half of the nineteenth century brought a period of upheaval in the young republic, reverberating through culture, politics, and economy. Americans industrialized and fought a war not so much between the states as between the smokestacks and steel of the North and the slave-based feudal agriculture of the South. We admitted an unprecedented flow of migrants from the Old Country and Asia, just as we engaged in an unprecedented internal migration of people headed for the gold fields, first of the West Coast, then of the Black Hills and Rockies. We railroaded our way to Manifest Destiny and sent the economy through a series of massive, nationwide panics and booms and busts in the process. Yet in this great sweep of continental, even global, forces, I choose to single out two developments that dictated beyond a doubt that the experiment in a bison-based plains culture would be cut short. The first development is obscure and technological; the second is a social sea change recognizable to any American who has lived during the first few years of the twenty-first century.

Industrialization was the root cause of rapid social change in the United States in the mid-nineteenth century. It was above all a revolution of power, steam engines turning wheels. Coal turned the steam engines so that belts—leather belts—could turn wheels. There was an enormous demand for leather that made tanning the fifth-largest industry in the United States by 1850. It was centered in New York and Pennsylvania, largely because of access to trees in the Adirondacks; the eastern hemlock was a prime source of tannin, from which the process of tanning hides gets its name. Indeed, the tanning industry was a prime sponsor of the deforestation that marked the period, as it was of stench and water pollution.

Its basic resource was cattle hides, and by 1870 the demand had outstripped supply. The domestic industry was running on cattle hides imported from another neo-European grassland, the pampas of South America. The tanners were well aware of a seemingly endless supply of bison hides, but no one had developed a method of stripping the extraordinarily dense coat of hair, which would allow factories to tan those hides. The supply crunch, however, drove intense and successful experimentation. Tanners hit on the solution of soaking the hides in lime. This unique process made unusually elastic leather. As a result, tanned bison hides made even better drive belts than cattle hides did.

At the same time, industrialism refined machine tools, which in turn created more accurate repeating rifles, which then allowed the relatively unskilled to wreak wholesale slaughter on a scale that no nomadic hunter-gatherer could have imagined. Immigration and the end of the Civil War both produced a glut of young men looking for adventure and fortune. And finally, the steel rails were snaking across the continent, giving hunters a way to ship the mountains of hides. The railroads had made it to the edge of the southern plains in Kansas and on to Denver by 1870, concentrating the hide hunters there. The southern plains herd was the first to go. The Northern Pacific had pushed its way to Glendive, Montana, by 1879, prefacing the demise of the northern herd. It would be wiped out in seven years. (See figure 1.)

The facilitated hide business quickly removed a key control on the level of slaughter. No longer did the business depend on a limiting infrastructure: the number of women available to process hides to robes. Now the limit was the number a team of hunters could shoot, skin,

THE LAST BUFFALO.

"Don't shoot, my good fellow! Here, take my 'robe,' save your ammunition, and let me go in peace."

Figure 1. Cartoon by Thomas Nast from Harper's Weekly, *June 6, 1874.*

and haul to the railhead. Calculations placed native bison use at about six per person per year, and even then that level of harvest was at the raw edge of sustainability. Now a team of three or four hide hunters typically slaughtered fifty to seventy bison *per day*. Economic determinism would suggest that this level of slaughter was sufficient to cause the bison's demise, but an interesting and countervailing social force is a telling sidebar to the economic story. The public was, in fact, generally aware of the tragedy that was playing out on the plains, and they applied intense political pressure to stop it.

By 1870, a generation's worth of dire warnings had been relayed to easterners, beginning with those of both Catlin and Prince Maximilian. Both of their reports came from the heart of the northern plains, as did a more expert assessment in the early 1870s. The noted biologist George Bird Grinnell was part of a government survey party that steamed up the Missouri in 1875, then climbed off the boat and up onto the prairie in the very heart of the Missouri Breaks. The party worked its way southwest to the area that is now Yellowstone National Park, and Grinnell conducted a thorough survey of wildlife that stands today as a sort of presettlement catalog. His experience was varied. Nonetheless, his short letter of transmittal with his report dwelled on just one point:

> It may not be out of place here, to call your attention to the terrible destruction of large game, for their hides alone, which is constantly going on in those portions of Montana and Wyoming through which we passed. Buffalo, elk, mule-deer and antelope are being slaughtered by thousands each year, without regard to age or sex, at all seasons. Of the vast majority of the animals killed, the hide only is taken. Females of all these species are as eagerly pursued in the spring, when just about to bring forth their young, as at any other time.
>
> It is estimated that during the winter of 1875–76 not less than 3,000 elk were killed for their hides alone in the valley of the Yellowstone, between the mouth of Trail Creek and the Hot Springs. If this be true,

what must have been the numbers for both Territories? Buffalo and mule deer suffer even more severely than the elk, and antelope nearly as much. The Territories referred to have game laws, but, of course, they are imperfect, and cannot, in the present condition of the country, be enforced. Much, however, might be done to prevent the reckless destruction of the animals to which I referred, by the officers stationed on the frontier, and a little exertion in this direction would be well repaid by the increase of large game in the vicinity of the posts where it is not unnecessarily and wantonly destroyed.[17]

Indeed, there is some indication that the officers stationed on the frontier were of a mind to help correct the situation, and not just for bison. By now, the fates of both bison and Indian were linked in the American imagination, as they were in economic fact. Grinnell's report was attached to that of Col. William Ludlow, making it part of an official investigation by the U.S. Army. The historian Richard White argues that this was not an isolated event for the army, which was, at the time, a sort of stabilizing buffer between white boomers and the Indians in the hide trade.[18]

White argues that while some generals did indeed hate Indians, a long list of "humanitarian generals," such as John Pope, George Crook, Oliver O. Howard, and John E. Wool, saw their role as protecting Indians from whites. Removing Indians from the depredations of whites was the prime rationalization for the reservation system, but it was actually more than rationalization. Historian White cites the cases of California and Oregon, where white settlers offered bounties, hired Indian hunters (i.e., people who hunted and killed Indians, as opposed to hunters who were Indians), and lynched their Indian neighbors by the thousands. Says the historian, "Whites killed an estimated 4,500 Indians in California between 1848 and 1880. This is the minimal estimate, for many attacks certainly were unrecorded. Nor does the number include those Indians whom violence drove away to starve or die of disease. Most of those killed died at the hands of civilians, not soldiers."[19]

The army's streak of protectiveness toward both Indians and bison spread to civilians in the East. By the end of the Civil War, this protectiveness had become a potent political force. The officers who witnessed the slaughter on the plains communicated directly with a growing animal protection movement in the Northeast.

The drive to protect animals from cruelty had begun, like industrialism, in Britain in the early nineteenth century. It spread to the United States then, but didn't really become prominent until after the Civil War. In both countries, the movement was urban, middle-class, and largely feminine, and in both it preceded but also fueled movements to prevent cruelty to humans. Worries about animal rights came before abolition, child labor laws, and especially protests over genocide against Native Americans. Isenberg says this was a direct result of urbanization: "Nearly all reformers were middle-class city dwellers. Critical and fearful of urban mechanization and poverty, they rued the loss of rural innocence, particularly farmers' solicitude for their animals."[20]

Henry Bergh, son of a wealthy shipbuilder, founded the Society for the Prevention of Cruelty to Animals in New York in 1866. He took up the cause of bison in the early '70s after contact from military officers and a group of women from Freeport, Illinois. The eastern press also took up the cause of bison, especially *Harper's Weekly* and the *New York Times*, but both were even more at the forefront of a drive to protect Indians. This was an extension of the sentiments the nation had developed during the Civil War. Wrote the *Times:* "We have long been doing justice to the negro. Is it not almost time to see what we can do for the Indian?"[21]

The two issues quickly conjoined, for instance, with arguments from *Harper's* that the violence of the Indians on the plains and the racial warfare against them were direct results of the desperation of Indians deprived of the basis of their economy, the bison. Preservation of the bison was a way to preserve peace long enough for Indians to become assimilated into the spreading agrarian culture, ignoring, of course, their prior assimilation into the dominant culture's fur trade on the plains for nearly a century.

Eventually, the political forces converged in the character of Representative Greenburg Lafayette Fort, a Republican from Illinois. He introduced bills in both 1874 and 1876 that, among other measures, such as restoring reservation rights to some tribes, made it illegal for anyone other than an Indian to kill a female bison in any of the U.S. territories. Fort was a quixotic character, regarded as something of a crank in Congress, but his bills were taken seriously by most. Had the Grant administration taken them seriously, the plains could well have had a very different history. Both the Senate and House passed his 1874 bill. The House passed the 1876 version. President Ulysses Grant pocket-vetoed the 1874 bill, largely as a result of his stubborn secretary of interior, Columbus Delano. Among the other prominent corruptions of the administration, some people in it or at least connected to it—the Haliburtons of the day—were getting rich off beef contracts to Indian reservations.

But more overtly, those opposing Fort had begun arguing specifically that wiping out the bison would force the Indians into dependency and onto reservations. Historians have long argued whether the demise of the bison was the result of simple economic forces or the result of deliberate government policy rooted in racism. It's difficult to see why that argument exists, given the written record. Delano himself was specific on this point. He wrote that he would not "seriously regret the total disappearance of the buffalo from our western prairies, in its effect on the Indians, regarding it rather as a means of hastening their sense of dependence upon the products of the soil and their labors."[22] Westerners put it more bluntly. Colonel Richard Irving Dodge said, "Kill every buffalo you can; every buffalo dead is an Indian gone."[23]

This whole debate may well have had a very different outcome had not events tipped the balance in the opposite direction. The debate that existed into 1876 was simply not possible after late June of that year, when a confederation of plains tribes annihilated General George Armstrong Custer's troops at the Little Bighorn. The nation locked its vision onto imagined images of that event, literally, lurid paintings that became a standard fixture in barrooms and public spaces across the country, analogous to the way that "United We Stand" bumper stickers proliferated after September 11, 2001. The art shared many bumper-sticker qualities, including some shortchanging of the facts.

The writer Evan S. Connell describes the flow of paintings in detail in *Son of the Morning Star*, his important account of this turning point in western history. The artists' response to the massacre was almost immediate, with the first and prototypical painting reproduced in the New York *Daily Graphic* on July 19, 1876, less than a month after the event depicted. Of course, none of the artists had seen the battle or even knew what Custer looked like on that day, so they were free to deliver us a young, proud god with flowing mane and erect sword. Writes Connell, "Artists who set out to recreate a unit of the nineteenth century United States Army such as the Seventh Cavalry therefore had a problem. A short-haired general commanding what might be mistaken for a limping, drunken mob of itinerant farmhands would be altogether unsatisfactory. What the public has a right to expect is a flaxen-haired, saber-wielding general and his valiant troopers in neat blue uniforms trapped hopelessly within a constricting circle of bronze savages wearing enormous feather bonnets and waving tomahawks."[24] In fact, Connell meticulously documents the less flattering image, but the public was given the flag-waving version in a series of famous paintings. No less a thinker than Walt Whitman was so taken with one such painting that he concluded, "Nothing in the books like it, nothing in Homer, nothing in Shakespeare; more grim and sublime than either, all native, all our own and all a fact."[25]

The images of Custer's fall inspired a reaction that almost instantly reversed the national mood, just as did the images of the World Trade Center's twin towers falling in our time. After the Little Bighorn, the humanitarian sentiments toward natives collapsed, just as a present-day reaction allows this nation to countenance widespread and systematic torture of people we regard as uncivilized and to countenance civilian deaths by the hundreds of thousands. Underneath the fury and racism, though, lay a hard economic fact: Our nation became fully resolved to conquer the West and the resources it held.

Even those who lamented the demise of the bison acknowledged this as the cost of "progress." The naturalist William Hornaday, who had issued some of the alarms over the slaughter, reacted to the bison's demise by traveling to Montana in 1886 and killing the last one he could find on a stretch of land at the edge of the Missouri Breaks. George Bird Grinnell, John Muir, and Ernest Thompson Seton, conservationists every one, weighed in with the sober assessment that the extermination of the bison was necessary to spread civilization.[26] Theodore Roosevelt, who, along with Grinnell, would more or less invent conservation in the United States, agreed with this notion, but still it was the bison that drew him as a young New York assemblyman to the West. He said he wanted to kill one "while there were still buffalo left to shoot."[27] In September 1883, just seven years after Custer fell, a twenty-five-year-old Theodore Roosevelt made the train trip west to Medora, South Dakota, on Montana's eastern edge. After a long hunt plagued by the rigors of fall weather, TR finally scored; he describes it in one of his many books, *The Lordly Buffalo:*

There below me, not fifty yards off, was a great bison bull. He was walking alone, grazing as he walked. His glossy fall coat was in fine trim and shone in the rays of the sun, while his pride of bearing showed him to be in the lusty vigor of his prime. As I rose above the crest of the hill, he held up his head and cocked his tail to the air. Before he could go off, I put the bullet in behind his shoulder. The wound was an almost immediately fatal one, yet with surprising agility for so large and cumbersome an animal, he bounded up the opposite side of the ravine . . . and disappeared over the ridge at a lumbering gallop, the blood pouring from his mouth and nostrils. We knew he could not go far, and trotted leisurely along his bloody trail.[28]

TR's first encounter with the West produced more than a wall-mount bison head. The landscape almost immediately laid a claim to him, so much so that when, a few years later, his wife and mother died, both within twenty-four hours, he retreated again to the Badlands to grieve and, by his own accounts, build the personal strengths, the character of one our nation's most remarkable and enigmatic figures. Much of this explains why this privileged, Harvard-educated knickerbocker would have more to do with the shape of the modern West than any other president, save his young cousin. But more concretely, TR made a decision during that 1883 visit that set him on a course parallel to that of many of the young and privileged around the globe: He decided to become a rancher.

Three

PROPERTY WAS THEFT

With this orgy of destruction, the natural economy of the northern Great Plains perished, and none of white man's devices has yet sufficed to restore the perfect balance of Nature, man and food, in this grim and unforgiving land.

— *Joseph Kinsey Howard*, Montana

Everywhere the Montanan is surrounded by his real heritage. Almost nowhere will he recognize it.

— *K. Ross Toole*, Montana

The heart of the Missouri Breaks today is the most depopulated stretch of a depopulated empty landscape. The Breaks themselves are parallel bands of land, each maybe two miles or five miles wide, undulating parallel to the lazy, muddy bends of the Missouri River. They form a hilled and hummocky terrain, slit and trenched by ancient watercourses. Their geology records the power and glory of floods. The Missouri's bed was created by the leading edge of the continental ice sheet, then tortured and sculpted to its present form first by local glacial melt and later by cataclysmic floods from rapid melt in the Rocky Mountains, a couple hundred miles west.

One can quickly read this fluid history on the present face of the land. The relatively flat prairie, seemingly infinite, stretches to the edge of the Breaks, then a sudden drop occurs, with the prairie's edge remaining several hundred feet above the river's surface. From the top edge, one shares the view of the river below with golden eagles, common here. Their flight gives their perspective no great advantage over that of the pedestrian.

Often no artifact appears, either in Breaks below or in prairie behind. I usually have to leave the bench, walk down an ancient gully to river's edge, cross a two-track jeep road, and walk farther still before stumbling on the occasional ruin of a settler's cabin in the river's broad valley—bleached-out boards of a shack, a few rusting pipes, and a fallen pole fence of a corral. If I were to wander this place long enough, I would find the ruins of entire towns, their dance halls and bars, now just the few logs spared by rot and seasonal floods. This depopulated portion of the landscape was once the most densely settled spot in the region and would remain so until the New Deal sent the people packing.

Biologists often refer to the edge effect, a flurry of life that obtains where one ecotype shifts to another. Clearly, the Missouri was an edge during glaciation; a more dramatic shift could not be imagined, with an ice sheet on the north side and woolly mammoths and mammoth-hunting people frequenting the other. But it remained a cultural edge between whites and natives, outlaws and settlers, thieves and vigilantes well into the twentieth century, with a particular violence that respects the geological precedent. Many of these conflicts were rooted in the place's rapidly shifting economies.

In the beginning of white settlement, the two towns a couple of miles from what is now a legally designated wilderness area were Carroll and Rocky Point. The former was a port of sorts, beginning service in the late 1860s, and was officially designated a town in 1873, three years before Custer and company would leave their bones at the Little Bighorn. Carroll was the invention of capitalists under contract to the Northern Pacific Railroad, which had to ship goods brought up the Missouri River to its railhead at Corinne, Utah. The Carroll road was meant to be an alternate route for hauling goods by wagon to the booming gold and silver mines along the Rockies, especially at Helena, today the state's capital. Before Carroll, all these goods traveled south out of Fort Benton, Prince Maximilian's way station farther upstream, but a set of rapids between Carroll and Fort Benton made that stretch unnavigable at low water. Carroll was born of the need for year-round shipping.[1]

The Missouri was then mainly used for transportation, and the land around it for wood to fuel the steamboats. Logging seems laughable today, only four or five miles off the river. The prairie contains no trees, but the steep slopes of the Breaks are whiskered with stubby pine, mostly stunted ponderosa, and the bottomlands grow cottonwood, probably the world's worst firewood. Other than the decimation of wildlife, probably the biggest environmental impact of the fur trade in the plains was the deforestation of riparian areas, which never held much of a forest to begin with. The original entrepreneurs here were known as "woodhawks," I'd like to think because they had to go up on the hills among the hawks to get much wood.

The Breaks also drew a fair number of trappers, first of bison, deer, elk, beaver, and bighorn sheep. Those workers, however, were forced to transition as the slaughter wound down to its dismal conclusion; extinction founded an era of scavengers. Wolves proliferated on the abandoned carcasses, so Rocky Point especially became known as a wolfer's town, its primary industry being the killing of wolves for both bounty and hides. Bone pickers skulked in behind the wolfers. The bison skeletons bleaching on the plains became valuable once the railroads pushed in. The trains carried them east to be ground for fertilizer. Malta, the town at the north edge of the Breaks—we will visit it often in the course of this tale—was founded by bone pickers in 1887.

Meanwhile, settlement, especially the attempt to lure railroads, required a certain amount of revision of treaties with the Indians, by now far more destitute than when Catlin first saw them only forty years before. Fewer bison remained by the early 1870s, and a declining fur trade was being prosecuted mostly by whites. The Indians were, as the British say, redundant.

The corrupt Grant administration began dealing with Indians in 1871 through executive order. The administration exercised this power in 1874 by making the Missouri River the southern boundary of Indian territory, then, only a year later, further reducing the reservation of the Blackfeet to push them off their best hunting grounds. The government professed to remedy the poverty it created with these land grabs by providing the Indians with beef, but then it let the contracts to supply the beef to Grant's cronies, who as often as not took the government's money, then sold the beef elsewhere.

During this time, the Missouri took its role as the edge of separate worlds seriously; whites who were not wolfers lived along the river and made ends meet by trading whiskey and firearms to the Indians. Horse thievery, long an economic force among Indians on the plains, transitioned to whites, just as the fur trade had. The rough country of the Breaks and their status as edge of the Indian world made them an ideal hideout for outlaws, then engaged in horse theft. The gangs stole horses from settlers in the Dakotas and Wyoming, then ran them north into Canada for sale. Once in Canada, they would reverse the process, re-creating a new demand for stolen horses.

Wolfers, whiskey traders, woodhawks, horse thieves, and bone pickers—this was plains society as Granville Stuart found it when he came into the country in 1880. Stuart and his colleagues would, in six short years, effect the most sweeping and lasting social and environmental upheaval that ever occurred on Montana's plains. Stuart was not the first man to run cattle here, but he is the most remembered, largely because he was self-conscious enough about his role as a pioneer to write about it. He began preening for his story, in fact, before coming to the Breaks. Stuart arrived in Virginia City, in western Montana, and staked mining claims in 1864. He reports that in the same year, the town organized and, only a few months into its history, formed a historical society, with Stuart as secretary. That is, recording history was held as a priority of the town with less than a year of white history.

Stuart carried on in that role throughout his life and wrote a two-volume memoir, the second volume of which, *Pioneering in Montana: The Making of a State, 1864–1887*, presents us with much of the detail we know of early ranching years and also places us on a slippery slope. Stuart was an extremely enigmatic character. For instance, he could be vituperatively racist in print but never mentions he was married to an Indian woman. The pioneers were fallible narrators, a fact well documented. The historian Clyde Milner interviewed and compiled late-life stories of a series of Montana pioneers, then compared them with the diaries of those same people and with other written accounts of the time.[2] Not surprisingly, he found many discrepancies, such as claims of witnessing certain events that the narrators could not have witnessed, Indian attacks when there were none. Intriguingly, though, this was not a simple matter of getting facts wrong. From these fallible accounts, a remarkably intricate collective story emerges to show details shared among the versions. That is, the collective story of pioneers overshadowed their personal stories. Put another way, Milner's experience parallels the famous scene that ends the western film *The Man Who Shot Liberty Valance*: When facts contradict the myth, we westerners stick with the myth.

Slippery slope or not, though, Stuart's account tells us he quickly gave up mining, finding it more lucrative to supply the mining camps with cattle. By the end of the 1870s, his herds and others had badly overgrazed the intermontane valleys of the Rockies, so Stuart himself set out on a months-long trip on horseback, scouting the prairies for good grass. He found a spot that suited him and, in the fall of 1880, drove a herd through the Judith Gap and built a ranch at the foot of the Judith Mountains near the present-day town of Lewistown. That site was then a Metis settlement, people Stuart refers to as "breeds."

By 1884, Stuart had become an officer in the Montana Stock Growers Association, which claimed 429 members at its meeting that year at Miles City. Clearly, the cattle business had boomed in four years. Included in the membership were the Marquis de Mores and Theodore Roosevelt. Stuart mentions their presence but leaves out a detail recorded by Roosevelt's biographer, Edmund Morris. De Mores and Roosevelt had come to Miles City to ask to be included in a project of Stuart's, a vigilante posse that targeted horse thieves and cattle rustlers. Morris says Stuart refused on account of the two men's social prominence, which would have compromised Stuart's need for discretion. Stuart did not need his story repeatedly filtered through TR's even-then famous and constantly wagging teeth.[3]

From the cattlemen's perspective, the rustling was simple theft costing them their profits, but this neglects the fact that the cattlemen themselves owned not a blade of the grass that fattened their cattle, nor did they own the land beneath. They were simply taking what was there for the taking, as were the horse thieves. The vigilantes were not so much rounding up thieves as they were eliminating their economic competition.

Whatever the case, Stuart did unleash his vigilantes to commit what the historian Richard White calls the worst outbreak of vigilante violence in the West. The tallies vary, but White says that a summer's worth of hangings, shootings, and burnings in the Missouri Breaks killed thirty-five men, among them a man named Dixie Burr. Stuart does not tell us about this man, but Burr was, in fact, his nephew.[4] Stuart himself says there were but fourteen deaths and recounts them with enough detail to convince us of his presence at them. The violence all centered along the Missouri, near the mouth of the Musselshell River and at the town of Rocky Point, which by then was regarded as simply a horse thieves' town.

The character of this violence is best revealed in a story told by an old cowboy, Bill Armington, in an oral history interview conducted in the 1950s. Armington lived most of his life in the Breaks and was a friend of Stuart's son, Charlie:

Charlie [Stuart] told me another good one one time. About when the horse thieves was working on them over there quite a bit and Fergus and Stuart—Granville Stuart—and some of them belonged to the Masonic Lodge and got together and organized the vigilantes. They'd give these guys a trial amongst themselves, you know, they knew the guys that was working on them, and one of the ring leaders was a feller called Fiddling Sam, Sam MacKenzie. Of course, Charlie didn't know anything about that—he was just a young feller—but he remembered the deal all right. Anyway, one morning, I think the second or third of July, a feller rode into the ranch and said, "I see old Fiddling Sam's back." And they had him on a blacklist. He was one of the leaders. He said the old man pricked up his ears and said, "How do you know he's back?" and he said, "I just come from a dance over here. He played for the dance last night." And so he said the old man went out and caught a horse and pulled out. And so they had a Fourth of July celebration at Maiden, a little mining town close to Fort McGinnis, and Charlie Stuart and another young feller and a couple of girls were going to this celebration and they come around the bend of the creek, and here they see old Fiddling Sam hanging on the tree. Stuart said his old neck was stretched out about that far and all slumped down, and they all pulled up and took a look at him and one of these fellers with him got his wind and said, "I wonder if old Sam's got any matches. I ain't had a smoke for the last two or three miles." So he was riding kind of a gentle horse, and he spurred him up close to old Fiddling Sam and reached in his vest pocket and got some matches, and so Stuart rode up about that time and said, "Wonder if the old son-of-a-gun's got any money." He had moccasins on and he patted the bottom of his feet and he felt money rattling, so they took his moccasins off and they took his matches and his money and went on to the Fourth of July celebration.[5]

The vigilantes, known as "Stuart's stranglers," probably recorded their exploits in such detail because the action taken was against whites. Likely there was even more freelance murder directed against Indians but deemed not worth mentioning. We do get some snippets, though. A local paper, the *Mineral Argus*, quoted a correspondent as spotting seven Indians hanging in cottonwoods in the Musselshell Valley. The report began: "There are seven good Indians on Cottonwood Creek."[6]

Stuart himself clarifies his attitudes toward the natives and their rights to their land:

> At this time, 1880–81, the management of our Indian affairs was about as bad as it could well be, and it was idle for us to hope for relief from wrongs that would have made Henry Ward Beecher swear like a trooper.
>
> Let me review this delectable system and how it worked. First the government sets apart for each tribe enough of the choicest land to make a state; larger in fact than many of the older states in the Union, upon which the white man in search of homes may not put his foot, or even allow his domestic animals to feed upon the grasses which there grow up and decay without benefit to anyone, but the Indian who makes no use of this vast domain is allowed to leave at his own sweet will, and to stay away as long as he pleases and this he does for the well-known purpose of stealing the white men's horses, eating his cattle and robbing his cabin.[7]

These were not, however, idle musings but, according to Stuart's report, sentiments shared by the cattlemen's association. In the first years of its existence, the association met with Martin Maginnis, the territory's representative in Washington DC, to demand that the government appropriate "several millions" of dollars to protect the stockmen's interest. Writes Stuart, "If the government refused to extend its strong arm for the protection of the citizens of northern Montana, there was no recourse left them but to protect their own property and it was natural that they should do so."[8]

Indians and horse thieves were, however, not the cattlemen's worst problem. Their real enemies were one another. The early 1880s brought a massive influx of cattle onto the northern range, and not just from western Montana. Drovers pushed longhorns north from Texas and shorthorns from Oregon and Washington. The flow consisted not only of animals but also of capital. De Mores is a good example, a French noblemen who had connections to New York society and had migrated to the frontier to make his fortune. Similarly, in the Breaks, the storied Matador Ranch, now owned by the Nature Conservancy, was a venture of capitalists from the British Isles.

Montana historians Michael Malone, Richard B. Roeder, and William L. Lang have written of this period:

> By the later 1870s, so much American meat was being imported into the British Isles that a delegation from the Royal Agricultural Commission conducted a full investigation of the western cattle industry. Its report, brimming with enthusiasms over the profit potential of the Plains grasslands, persuaded many British capitalists to invest in livestock. Englishmen controlled many prominent firms, such as the N-F ranch on the lower Musselshell, the Montana Sheep and Cattle Company, Ltd., and the Chalk Buttes Ranch and Cattle Company, Ltd. Although the enormous Matador outfit was Texas-based, Scottish investors actually owned it.[9]

The implications of this boom were both economic and environmental, both aspects based in the government ownership of the open range. The cattlemen appropriated the grass without paying for it. In fairness, however, policy made it nearly impossible for them to buy it. The Homestead Act of 1862 said the public domain had only one purpose: to be permanently settled and worked by yeoman farmers, on 160-acre allotments. The period of the open range was not at all unique to the northern plains or even to the West in general. Virtually every advance of settlement west of the Allegheny Mountains had been preceded by a period of free-range grazing, to the point that the government regarded this as the natural course of events. The cattlemen were simply using the land temporarily until the real stalwarts of the American economy showed up with their plows, and in the interim the graziers could use it as they pleased.

The cattle boom and lack of control quickly led to overgrazing; land was completely stripped of grass cover and especially of riparian vegetation, which shelters streams and protects against erosion. All of this was exacerbated by a defensive technique common to the ranchers: They deliberately overgrazed land they occupied as a sort of scorched-earth policy; it prevented other herds from moving into their territory.

Still, they prospered, largely because of a short and unusual stretch of forgiving weather. A lot of people made a lot of money, a phenomenon that enticed the financially naive Theodore Roosevelt to invest a dangerously huge portion of his family fortune in a ranch on the Little Missouri in the 1880s. He was not alone in making this kind of investment, nor would he be alone in paying nature's bill, which came due after 1886. A drought occurred in the summer of that year, leaving the herds weakened and facing what would be the most severe winter anyone could remember. No other season has been so catastrophic for ranching, the first and worst year of a period still known as the big die-ups. Those enormous herds that had flooded the newly opened range were made up of beasts unaccustomed to such beastly weather, especially the Texas longhorns. Their normal surrounds were more temperate, but also their bodies, smaller than those of modern cattle bred for temperate regions, rapidly lost heat because of the ratio of mass to surface area.

Its hard to know exactly how many cattle died that winter, but the generally accepted number is about 60 percent of the herds, more than 350,000 animals. Several historians caution that corporate chicanery inflates this number, because managers took advantage of the general die-off to balance some previously inflated accounts. For instance, one manager claimed to have lost 125 percent of his herd: 75 percent of his steers and 50 percent of his cows. Personal accounts make it clear, though, that a real and sobering disaster did occur. Gladys Miller, a historian of Phillips County, wrote:

> It was impossible for the cattle to reach the grass under the snow. They started back to Texas. They drifted down to the Milk River where they staid [sic] until the river froze solid so they could cross. They ate willows as big as a man's wrist. Every morning, Mr. Hedges [the rancher

Miller interviewed] had to roll dead cattle from his shed door. The poor beasties froze and starved, their heads turned towards Texas. In the spring they were still standing until the spring sun thawed out their carcasses and they fell down. Splinters of wood a foot long were sticking through their stomachs.[10]

Spring throughout the plains that year brought omnipresent evidence of disaster. Roosevelt, riding into Medora to inspect his losses, reported finding one carcass suspended in a cottonwood tree, where it had been standing atop a snowdrift when it died. Everywhere a sort of hydrology of carcasses formed; rows of them marked the flow of melt from snowdrifts, then floods of them swept from riverbanks until the region's watercourses flowed with dead cattle. One rancher remembered it as a thirsty spring, simply because the carcasses fouled all waters.

Only six years into the period of the open range, the cattle industry had reworked the landscape, then had been reworked by it. It is difficult to imagine a more momentous six years on the plains since the glaciers retreated. Stuart provides the summary:

It would be impossible to make persons not present on the Montana cattle ranges realize the rapid change that took place on the ranges in two years. In 1880 the country was practically uninhabited. One could travel for miles without seeing so much as a trapper's bivouac. Thousands of buffaloes darkened the rolling plains. There were deer, antelope, elk, wolves, and coyotes on every hill and in every ravine and thicket. In the whole territory of Montana there were but two hundred and fifty thousand head of cattle, including dairy cattle and work oxen.

In the fall of 1883 there was not one buffalo roaming on the range and the antelope, elk, and deer were indeed scarce. In 1880 no one had heard tell of the cowboy "in this niche of the woods," and Charlie Russell had made no pictures of them; but in the fall of 1883 there were six hundred thousand head of cattle on the range. The cowboy[s], with leather chaps, wide hats, gay handkerchiefs, clanking silver spurs, and skin-fitting high-heeled boots were no longer a novelty, but had become an institution.[11]

Stuart put his losses at 65 percent during the big die-ups, a blow that would forever sour him, the quintessential cattleman, on running cattle on the open range. He wrote, "A business that had been fascinating to me before suddenly became distasteful. I wanted no more of it. I never wanted to own again an animal that I could not feed and shelter."[12] Stuart the strangler and rancher left the range and the cattle business, eventually to work as the city librarian in the mountain mining town of Butte.

∽

The blow of the severe winter notwithstanding, one school of economic thought would argue that the big die-ups were the best example of a "tragedy of the commons." In fact, Garret Hardin, who coined the term, usually cited grazing systems in illustrating the phenomenon, because grazing land, not just in the American West but throughout Europe and the neo-Europes, has often been held in common, in contrast to farm plots. In its initial meaning, "the commons" referred to grazing land. Hardin's argument is that an individual using a common resource has no incentive to conserve that resource. He has every incentive to overgraze; if he doesn't, one of his neighbors will. That reasoning was implicit among western cattlemen. Many of Hardin's proponents—more aptly called disciples for their near-religious fervor—have seized on this as an argument for private property; the owner of property does have incentives to conserve to ensure a stable future. We'll leave for a moment some of the more sophisticated economic arguments that counter this and simply note the empirical fact that plenty of private property, especially rangeland, is every bit as severely abused as the commons.

Still, I don't mean to be dismissive of this issue. This argument about private property has everything to do with the long-term history of the

West. In the end, the biggest failure of the West was not so much the Jeffersonian myth as it was the European notion of private property— a notion that is the bedrock belief of the increasingly red-state West but is inappropriate in the West to the point that it almost never exists or exists mostly in myth.

We need to table this discussion, though, until we examine another era on the Missouri Breaks, when the land was homesteaded and became private. At this point, we know that private property did not yet fit with the nation's plans for the West, at least as far as the cattlemen were concerned; rather, it was part of the nation's plans for the yeomen who were settling there. But also a good argument can be made that private property on the plains was not technically possible until barbed wire made it into the country.

The issue of fencing was not at all an idle question in the nineteenth century. It was, in fact, a subject for lively, front-page debate triggered by a Department of Agriculture report in 1871 that showed fencing to be the single most expensive piece of the nation's infrastructure. It placed the total value of the nation's fences at an astronomical $1.7 trillion, with annual interest costs and maintenance set at another $198 million. Those costs exceeded all the taxes in the nation then—federal, state, and local. One newspaper reported, "There is not a solitary county in any agricultural district of the Union in which fencing has not cost ten times as much as the value of the stock in such county."[13] This cost was a tax of sorts, a tax on the idea of private property. The price of a good fence is, as Robert Frost reported, the cost of being a good neighbor, which meant respecting borders.

Yet these costs accrued only in the East; while the costs were huge there, they were simply unbearable in the West. The USDA's 1871 report addresses the small and intensively productive forty-acre plots of eastern and midwestern yeomen. An eastern acre supports several cows, but in the West a single cow needs something like forty acres. If fencing was the cost of private property in the West, then the institution simply wouldn't bear the costs. To a certain extent, that shift in attitude, created by fundamental economics, is still with us. As Frost knew and as every eastern farmer knows, those fences keep one's livestock from destroying a neighbor's crops, so the farmer's first responsibility is to pen his animals. Many farming communities have farmers notorious for their lousy fences, and they are regarded as pariahs. In the West, though, that idea has been reversed and is encoded in law. In grazing states, Montana included, it is a landowner's responsibility to fence cattle *out.* That is, if a neighbor's cattle destroy a farmer's grain field, the farmer is legally at fault. Cows have rights of trespass.

Barbed wire, however, did allow an extension of the notion of private property. Invented in 1874 in De Kalb, Illinois, this cheap form of fencing had become common in the West by 1880. It was a tool ranchers could reach for when the scale of the tragedy of the commons became apparent by the mid-'80s. They still had no legal means to claim ownership of the range, but they nonetheless used barbed wire to close the commons. That is, they illegally fenced public lands. By 1902, ranchers had illegally fenced at least 3.5 million acres of the public domain.[14]

The cattle disasters of the 1880s were only the beginning of a long series of defeats brought on by the European tradition and land law's inability to factor in the harsh rule of aridity. But just as there was significant political support to protect bison and Indians after the Civil War, there was also a good bit of opposition to manifest plans for the West. The work of John Wesley Powell, a one-armed Civil War veteran and one of America's first systematic government scientists, was the main force of this opposition. Specifically, Powell warned that the prevailing condition of the West was aridity, and it would not tolerate the settlement patterns that had homesteaded lands farther east. Powell was shouted down by some of the very same forces that had also defeated the drive for better treatment of natives and wildlife. This was not a petty academic dispute. The Montana historian Joseph Kinsey Howard comments on the results of ignoring the West's most important visionary: "Thousands of men, women, and children have had their lives permanently blighted by poverty—hundreds have actually starved—thousands of head of livestock have perished, acres of soil have been lost or damaged since Powell presented his plans for the plains—because Congress and the American people paid no attention whatever."[15]

This discussion usually leads to Powell's correct assessment of the inadequacies of the Homestead Act, that yeomen farmers could not be expected to make a living on 160 acres of parched western dirt. His predictions, however, went further. For instance, he knew the value of rivers; he thought that settlement ought to be clustered along rivers and that the landscape's inhabitants ought to be politically organized according to watersheds, counties made up of river basins, as opposed to arbitrary quadrilaterals. He also understood that native peoples had made certain accommodations with the landscape and that white settlers ought to learn from them and work with them to develop a more fitting mode of living on this tough land.

Well before the big die-ups of the 1880s, Powell specifically warned against fencing livestock, that it would lead to overgrazing and erosion. His premonition rested on the understanding that the West is a landscape of motion. Its humans are nomadic and its animals, such as bison and elk, are migratory for a reason. Good fences might make good neighbors elsewhere, but here they trap animals in inevitable local disasters. Fences are simply the visible manifestation of our idea of private property. That venerated institution is inappropriate in the West. That's why it has largely been superseded, and its undoing began with the cattlemen.

They fenced as an attempt to impose private property and shortly thereafter began using the various homestead laws to gain control of relatively small plots of land. This was the beginning of the development of a hybrid system that quickly closed the open range. The ranchers claimed premium lands, premium even by Powell's standards, in that these plots lay along river bottoms. The extra moisture and shelter there allowed ranchers to grow and harvest hay, a form of farming, not ranching, and the hay would carry animals through the winter. In summer, cattle grazed the uplands, public lands too vast and arid for homesteads. The ranchers claimed plots of 160 and later 320 acres, specified by the Enlarged Homestead Act of 1909, but they in fact controlled much larger acreages of unsettled public lands.

E. Louise Peffer writes in her 1951 history of the closing of public lands, "The cattlemen resorted to every possible subterfuge and distortion of the laws to gain ownership of the land or—and this was more important—control over it through acquisition of water holes and land along the banks of streams."[16] The West had begun to understand that the battle was over not land but water, a battle that would escalate sharply in the early twentieth century, when the railroads, hope, and hucksterism brought carloads of farmers into the high plains.

Robert Coburn and B. D. Phillips were pioneering ranchers of the Missouri Breaks. Politically, the place is now organized as Phillips County, named for the latter rancher, the town of Malta being the county seat. Yet it's Coburn's trail we need to follow for a moment. He was of that first generation of pioneers, the sort that present-day ranchers like to claim as a direct ancestor, just as Boston Brahmins trace ancestry to the *Mayflower*. Yet Coburn did not spawn a long line of ranchers. His son, Wallace, abandoned ranching and its privations to become a movie star.

In 1916, Coburn the younger returned to the Breaks with a crew of silent film stars, Eddie Polo, Vivian Reed, Hallam Cooley, Roy Hanford, Frank Lanning, William Welsh, Noble Johnson, and Leo Willis, to shoot a western called *Bull's Eye*, which was released in 1918.[17] The western myth may be more palatable than the reality, but it also is more lucrative. Only a generation after the open-range era, some of the people who lived it realized this fact and began shaping that myth into the long strings of oaters, Wild West shows, dime novels, and coffee table books that probably have made a lot more money than cattle ever did. Certainly, the open-range cattlemen have lasted a lot longer on film and page than the six years that were their actual tenure on the northern plains. We do indeed prefer the myth when it conflicts with the facts, mostly because there's more money in it.

Four

FACE IT TO LIVE

The closing of the range came in spurts and was as much a response to an influx of farmers as it was an evolution of the cattle business itself, a groping for a way of life that would allow European culture a foothold in the Breaks. From the clean, well-lighted distance, it is easy to summarize this in so much academic language, but there was a human dimension that defies breezy summary. This revisionist history of mine necessarily prods those who romanticize and deify those pioneers today, but I need to acknowledge that the yeoman settlers were indeed a different sort. I am still not convinced the world is altogether better for their passing. I make this case with an account, taken from the archives of the *Phillips County News*, of a winter's event that occurred in 1906 and was told to the newspaper by a principal:

> On the 26th day of December, my brother Tim Hartman and I with 14–16 horse teams pulling six wagons left Malta for Zortman [about forty-five miles to the southwest]. The deep snow and the cold winds made a man stick out his chest and say, "Oh boy, I'll face it to live." The roads were very bad, a foot of snow and more falling and about 20 degrees below zero as we hit the trail for Malta.
>
> It continued to snow and grow colder until it was about 47 degrees below, when we reached Malta. On the 3rd of January we began load-

ing up at Malta. The supplies were for George Heath and Dave Cline, merchants at Zortman. There were also mining supplies and a load of 10,000 pounds of oats for the Ruby mine. Each mail brought in new orders for supplies, which we were forced to leave behind. As we were the only ones on the road at that time of year we kept adding to our weight and loaded out with our feed about 42,000 pounds.

With three feet of snow on the level we realized the impossibility of driving thirty head of horses as we had done before. We made a snow plow. Ed Martinson was driving it with four horses hitched to it. Hank Boe was driving one wagon and six horses, my brother, Tim Hartman was driving ten horses hitched to two wagons and a camp cart. Joe Mollette with William Hollenbeck each with two, six-horse teams completed the caravan. On January 12 we started for Zortman, the thermometer registered 57 degrees below. That was our coldest day, 90 degrees below—perhaps.

With the horses well fed and strong, mighty in pulling power, we started. Three days later we reached the ridge in sight of Malta. That was January 15. I fought with my own brother to keep him from freezing to death.

Where did we sleep? In the camp carts, three in a bed. Each camp had a good stove and wood to begin with. Who could believe that our breath would freeze to ice under the blankets? To keep our horses from the feed we camped in a circle and fed our horses outside using the wagons as a corral to keep them from our feed.

On the 16th, we pulled down on main Alkali Creek for the night. Henry Moore was driving the Zortman stage with Howard Seaford as a passenger. They were camped in a snowdrift about a mile and a half away. Nineteen miles with a sled was all he could make in a day. We were a full day crossing Alkali and getting to the south side of it. That was on the eighteenth of January. A week out, and we pulled up in reservoir coulee. That was the last day we used the snow plow as we had to break it up for wood.

The blizzard of Blizzards began. Dug our harness out of the snow and shoveled snow away to start our horses. There were big drifts everywhere. We fed the last of our hay there. We had fed altogether so far forty-two bales of hay. We found grass under the snow that our horses could paw. Two bites of snow to one of grass. Then we began to feed the Ruby Mining Company's oats.

We wormed our way around the snow drifts, guided by a man on horseback. Jan. 21, we reached the Hog ranch. We were twenty-eight miles out of Malta and ten days on the road. We were out of meat and potatoes and our canned goods were frozen. We made baking powder biscuits. We were out of coal and short of wood and began using fence posts for fuel. We were out in the west where men were men and women were governors.

January twenty-second another blizzard and still cold. We lost our horses in the night and found them around the haystacks on the Phillips ranch. As we turned them out in the night to rustle and it was such slow going, they would always go back to the same stack of hay. Freighters don't like to overdo, and always take their time, but we had to this time. January twenty-third and we pulled into the Parrott ranch hungry and bawling with the cold. One horse down in the snow and one in the ranch barn that we were asked to give a lift on. Stubborn critter absolutely wouldn't get up. We were told to leave her. One of our best horses got down in the ice and froze. Then we began to get short of Ruby's oats. The horses were getting lame and bleeding under the hoofs. Winds blew colder and colder.

January thirty-first and we pulled in Coburn's, asked for hay and were told to feed all we wanted. Left Coburn's for Bear Gulch Hill. Pulled onto its crest the night of Feb. 6. A chinook wind came that night. February seventh we pulled over the bare ground into Zortman, weary men and tired horses, twelve of the horses crippled, and one sack of oats left out of 13,000 pounds. The horses were turned loose until spring broke April tenth.

Were they glad to see us? Yes, for we had flour, sugar, coffee, and tea and oil for lights instead of candles. That winter made many a good man say, "I quit."[1]

Another rancher, William Dunbar gives a more concise account of that same winter: "I shoveled snow for the sheep to get grass. At night we took our bedrolls and lay on the snow among the sheep. I skinned 3,000 head in the spring."[2]

We may doubt Hartman's estimate of a ninety-degree-below night, but not fifty-six below. A U.S. Fish and Wildlife Service biologist working the Breaks in 2003 left his camp for the winter but also left behind a thermometer that would accurately log the winter's coldest moment. When he returned in the spring, the reading was fifty-six below.[3]

Five

ALL HELL NEEDS

Unless the government shall grant homestead rights, or donations of some kind, these prairies, with their gorgeous growth of flowers, their green carpeting, their lovely lawns and gentle slopes, will for centuries continue to be the home of the wild deer and wolf; their stillness will be undisturbed by the jocund song of the farmer, and their deep and fertile soil unbroken by the ploughshare. Something must be done to remedy this evil.

— *Representative Orlando B. Fickling, of Illinois*

There is an island of life at the center of the Missouri Breaks. Those same cottonwoods that stood as makeshift gibbets for horse thieves and shelter for wolfers and whiskey traders are now principally wildlife habitat. The ravines are alive with mule deer, elk, and cougars. The flats hold prairie dogs, pronghorn antelope, and burrowing owls in abundance. The heart of the Breaks is the 1.1-million-acre Charles M. Russell National Wildlife Refuge, named for the cowboy artist whose famous painting *The Last of the 5000*, or *Waiting for a Chinook*, documented in stark detail the die-ups of the 1880s.

The refuge is not so much a triumph for conservation as it is an accident of history. The twentieth century's history of the West is hydraulic. This arid place is ruled by water, and we who inhabit it have all learned the deep meaning of our credo: In the West, water runs uphill toward money. One of the pinnacles of this grand-scale manipulation was the construction of the Fort Peck Dam as a make-work project during the Great Depression. It was then the largest earth-filled dam on the planet. The government bought most of the land in the Breaks from the settlers who had clustered near the water, as John Wesley Powell had predicted. The part of it that never flooded became the wild refuge.

This was all the work of Franklin Roosevelt, but in a very real sense this was also the work of his distant cousin, the rancher who went broke in the big die-ups, who wanted to hang horse thieves in these very cottonwoods and, instead, became president. More than a tangling of the two Roosevelts' legacies is at issue. Just as the Russell Wildlife Refuge's history is wound up in landscape-scale waterworks, the history of conservation itself, even the very idea of conservation, is wound up in our society's abuse of the western landscape. Initially this landscape's conservation was not so much a reaction as it was an offshoot of our groping with the shortcomings of private property. All of this is linked to a tie between the Roosevelts that is stronger than blood. Both the conservation movement and our destruction of the West are direct products of the Progressive movement, an assertion here, but a primary argument of the rest of this book. The case begins here, during the interregnum between the death of the open range and the coming of the homesteaders. All of this story is written and readable on the landscape of the Missouri Breaks.

The homesteaders who arrived in the Breaks beginning about 1909 were the last of their line, a final exception to the rule that allows this bit of Montana to tell best our nation's seminal struggle with itself. By the time they arrived, the homestead movement was more or less dead. The act itself was the product of the Lincoln administration, but its spirit arose in the mind of Thomas Jefferson and with the concept of Manifest Destiny. Simply, Jefferson saw the North American continent as only the latest extension of Western, principally European, civilization and thought democracy would be possible in this nation only if it were tiled coast-to-coast with forty-acre parcels, each populated with a freeholder, a financially independent farmer secured to democracy by land. It is a notion that extends to the very roots of democracy itself, as it began with wheat farms along the Aegean Sea. Even the prescient Powell, in calling for a new mode of living in the West, saw his idea as a variation on a primal theme. He said, "It is thus that a new phase of Aryan civilization is being developed in the western half of America."[1]

Senator Thomas Hart Benton introduced a bill to create a homestead act in 1825, but it died in the developing storm over slavery. Congress feared it would extend slavery into an agrarian West. The Civil War ended that fear, and in 1864, Congress passed the Homestead Act. By then, it was an act applying almost exclusively to unsettled lands, that is, lands west of the Mississippi. From the beginning, some saw the unique problems that existed there. Foresight was not Powell's alone.

In 1875, only thirteen years after homesteading began, the Public Lands Office of the Department of the Interior reported, "Except in the immediate valleys of the mountain streams, where by dint of individual effort water may be diverted for irrigating purposes, title to the public lands cannot be honestly acquired under the homestead laws. That cultivation and improvement, which are required, and which are made to stand in the place of price, are impossible; and if attempted, are without result."[2] This statement demonstrates acres of prescience, especially in the phrases "water may be diverted" and "honestly acquired." But the main thrust here is that to perfect a homestead, that is, to gain title, people had to live on the land they settled, and it was becoming increasingly clear that conditions in the West did not allow this.

That same year, President Ulysses Grant visited the West and returned pronouncing much of it fit only for pasturage. That and for pillaging by his cronies, but in his pronouncement he was correct, and the country could have saved itself a great deal of heartache had it paid heed. By the end of the century, the failure of the Homestead Act was manifest. Most of the lands remained unclaimed; the majority of the claims filed were never perfected. That is, the settlers had "starved out," to use the local term.

In this atmosphere of dysfunction, the very purpose of the act became distorted. By 1909, the magazine *Outlook* would report: "It is popular to refer to these throngs as 'land hungry,' and to consider that they are eager to obtain homes. The fact is however, that by far the greater portion is made up of men well-to-do who are attracted by the chance of securing a valuable prize without risk. The day of real land hunger passed many years ago; what now exists is at basis money hunger."[3]

As we have seen, the void on the prairie left cattlemen to make do to secure the resources they needed for their industry. They, in fact, began using the Homestead Act to settle employees, naive settlers, and town drunks on claims, support them on those claims only long enough to perfect them, then "buy" the land. The widespread practice was known as "dummy entrymen." This played out on an even larger scale in the forested areas of the Rocky Mountains, where land could be claimed under a parallel to the Homestead Act, the Timber and Stone Act. For instance, the copper barons who ran the mines at Butte, Montana, needed firewood for smelters and timbers for shoring adits and shafts. Using dummy entrymen and outright timber theft, they amassed something like a half million acres of timber lands in western Montana, lands that remain in corporate control to this day.

Congress would respond to this growing dysfunction by passing the Enlarged Homestead Act of 1909 (also known as the Kinkaid Act), which doubled settlers' allotments to 320 acres and did allow some successful homesteading in some of the more arid areas. In particular, Nebraska drew a wave of settlers then called "Kinkaiders." Many of these failed, too, but not in the spectacular fashion of the rush that had hit the Missouri Breaks.

A major response to the West's settlement—namely, to the growing failure of it—occurred, however, even before the enactment of the Enlarged Homestead Act. On the one hand, this response manifested itself as a rush toward irrigation, and, on the other, it paradoxically founded the conservation movement. Theodore Roosevelt was directly responsible for both aspects, and not so much because of his sympathy for the plains as because of his fear over what was going on in the forests.

⌁

Had the term then existed, Roosevelt could have been called a conservationist long before he was president. He was an amateur naturalist even as a boy. His first writings were as a naturalist, dating to his "Natural History on Insects," which he wrote when he was nine years old. It was that same curiosity about wild things that first drew him to the West, and the West, in turn, welded his connection to the natural world.

He made a trip west in 1887, following the big die-ups, but noted then the destruction of wildlife almost more than the destruction of his herds and fortune. His biographer Edmund Morris writes:

> Last summer's overstockings, together with desperate foraging during the blizzards, had eroded the rich carpet of grass that once held the soil in place. Sour deposits of cow dung had poisoned the roots of the wild plum bushes, so that they no longer bore fruit; clear springs had been trampled into filthy sloughs; large tracts of land threatened to become desert. What had once been a teeming natural paradise, loud with snorts and splashings and drumming hooves, was now a waste of naked hills and silent ravines.
>
> It would be hard to imagine a sight more melancholy to Roosevelt, who professed to love the animals he killed.[4]

That last phrase suggests a paradox to some, but it wasn't one for Roosevelt and hasn't been for many others then and since. Modern political taxonomists would place him in the ranks of what are known as "hook-and-bullet" environmentalists, people who preserve not so much animals in general as game. In fact, "in the ranks" understates the case. He founded the school of thought.

Returning from that forlorn trip west, Roosevelt, then only twenty-nine, gathered together a dozen wealthy and like-minded hunters at a dinner. Among them was George Bird Grinnell, the naturalist who had first visited the Breaks in 1875, then sounded the alarm we encountered in chapter 2 and had been amplifying it ever since, especially in his role as editor of *Forest and Stream*. Grinnell had become a close friend of Roosevelt's and was influential in molding him as a conservationist. The dinner led to the 1888 founding of the Boone and Crockett Club, with Roosevelt as president. The organization still exists, largely to rule over measurements of trophy game animals (a pursuit in which size does indeed matter), but also to do some conservation. It is headquartered today in my hometown, Missoula, Montana.

The choice of a name for the club reveals much about attitudes toward wildlife and nature. Davy Crockett and Daniel Boone were then legendary as woodsmen but also as soldiers serving Manifest Destiny. To Roosevelt, there was no irony in naming a conservation group for figureheads of the social force that exterminated most of the West's wildlife. He had a more complicated view. Hunting and roughing it in harsh wilderness constituted a sort of crucible that built the American character, especially its leaders. Roosevelt was first and foremost an elitist, and he meant to preserve those experiences for the elite as a sort of finishing school for wealthy young men, in his view, leaders. His conservation in no way sought to stem the onslaught of civilization, and he explicitly understood that destruction of wilderness and game was a part of that process. He and his colleagues simply meant to set aside some areas where the "manly" (his word) experience of hunting could be preserved for the elite.

This contradiction would be preserved when some of these same people, including Grinnell (who had by then founded the Audubon

Society), joined with naturalist William Hornaday to found the American Bison Society. This organization would go on to preserve the thin
numbers of surviving bison to allow, among other things, their recovery
in the Missouri Breaks as well as the recovery of the Breaks themselves,
which were no small matters. Nonetheless, it was an organization of
elitists when it began in 1908. Then U.S. president Theodore Roosevelt was also the Bison Society's honorary president. The bison was
the symbol of the American frontier, and the idea of frontier played
heavily in the driving mythology of the West then and now. Writes
the environmental historian Andrew C. Isenberg, "It was precisely their
[the Bison Society's members'] station in life—refined, cosmopolitan,
and comfortable, but also, they feared, overfed, effete and pampered—
that caused these privileged Easterners to romanticize the supposedly
hardier days when bison roamed the plains."[5]

Historian Frederick Jackson Turner had by then pronounced the
frontier closed, but it wasn't closed at all to Roosevelt, who sought to
extend it with unvarnished imperialist ambitions. So bent was he on
extending America's borders that he deliberately provoked the Spanish-
American War when he was an assistant secretary of the navy.

Modern biology understands that the issue of wildlife is secondary
to the preservation of habitat, and habitat is all about land. Despite his
high-profile role in the more limited conservation movement of his day,
Roosevelt thought this too. In this, he was well ahead of his time. The
truly bold initiatives of his administration involved the conservation of
landscapes. Specifically, he brought about the first deviation in the then-
single-minded American policy that all vacant land should be deeded
to settlers. He wedded conservation to the creation of a commons, to
public lands. To say we have vast areas of public lands in the West today because of Theodore Roosevelt is not overstatement. His achieve-
ment in creating public lands can be spelled out in acres. When Roosevelt left office there were 168 million acres of national forest; he
personally withdrew 141 million of those from development and homesteading during his tenure. He also created five new national parks, to-

taling 213,886 acres. Nothing like this had happened before, and nothing would again until the second Roosevelt.

But the background for this was the evolution of the term *conservation*, a word as protean then as now, then because of its newness, now because of its overuse and deliberate appropriation by the political newspeak that has poisoned our culture. The development that allowed conservation of public lands began, paradoxically, as an effort to extend irrigation to more western lands to allow more settlement.

Roosevelt was an accidental president, elevated to the position with the assassination of William McKinley in September 1901. He was already a national hero to some and suspect to many owing to his brash, straight ahead, bull-in-the-china-shop methods. He clamped onto issues like a rottweiler onto a leg, and the guardians (and beneficiaries) of the status quo knew this about him.

Yet he had an encyclopedic brain that reveled in analysis, debate, and dissection, and this is what showed in December of that same year, when the young president would deliver to Congress a crushing eighty-page book that was his State of the Union message. The practice then was to deliver the annual message in writing and have it read to both houses, an exercise that consumed more than a day. The weave of issues became apparent as Roosevelt wound from railroads through trust busting to a straightforward sermon on conservation. He bluntly called for the nation to embark on a program of protection of wildlife and habitat. Yet this was preface for something more concrete in his message: a call for conservation of water. He proposed the first national reclamation act, by which he meant vast federally funded irrigation projects for arid western valleys. His arguments about railroads, trusts, and the call for conservation all built to his keystone, the Reclamation Act, a law that the president would sign the following year, and it stands as one of his administration's pivotal accomplishments. Roosevelt himself believed this law was second only to the Homestead Act of 1862 in the American story.

"The western half of the United States would sustain a population greater than that of our whole country today if the waters that now run to waste were saved and used for irrigation," he wrote in his message to Congress. Or as westerners are fond of phrasing this same idea, "All hell needs is a little water." As a practical matter, this meant federal money for irrigation projects, a move Roosevelt felt necessary to stave off monopoly control of water in the West. In this, he was very much in line with the Jeffersonian ideal, despite his claim of despising Jefferson. Whatever the intent, the move touched off immediate speculation in the West. Gladys Miller, in her history of Phillips County, reports that the Lower Milk River Water Users Association formed in April, four months after Roosevelt's message to Congress. She writes: "As soon as the possibility of an irrigation project was foreseen, a mad scramble to secure lands along the river adjacent to these irrigation ditches began, and merchants, bankers, stockmen, and other business men joined the throng of settlers. This defeated the very purpose of the project, which was to give lands to farmers who could operate them profitably."[6]

In Malta, a sign went up in Richard Garland's store:

If we get the ditch, we'll all be rich,
We'll all have money galore,
If we don't get the ditch and don't get rich,
We'll live as we did before.[7]

Malta got the ditch and a dam at Dodson, a project whose real impact would not play out for another twenty-five years. But at the time, irrigation was the great hope of the West, and Teddy Roosevelt was its champion.

The back-door effect of his effort, however, was not so much in the construction of dams as it was a radical and complete departure from the nation's attitude toward public lands. Like John Wesley Powell, Roosevelt understood the lay of the land. If river valley settlers were to have a supply of water, upstream and upslope forested lands would need to be protected. Protection of headwater forests allows trees to shelter snow in spring and even into summer, metering a steady flow of clear, clean waters. That is to say, irrigation requires forest reserves.

Until that point, all lands, forested and otherwise, were meant for settlement, a problem, as we have seen, most often circumvented by theft. Also, the railroad land grants had given enormous swaths of timber to those very corporations Roosevelt was about to fight with his trust-busting activities, a defining theme of his administration. The Homestead Act of 1862 was designed to create democracy, but its forced fit with arid federal lands had created oligarchy and monopoly. The land that railroads were supposed to sell to settlers was instead aggregated and run as timber monopolies.

Roosevelt's conservation, at least in the beginning, was utilitarian in both the common and philosophical senses of the word. He was reserving forests for their utility, for use by settlers. In fact, his conservation would rest on the term *wise use*, a term appropriated and used without any intended irony today to justify the rapaciousness of the timber barons and strip miners of the West. In philosophical terms, though, the word means "greatest good for the greatest number of people," a page straight out of utilitarian philosophy. That is, it was wedded not only to Roosevelt's deeply embedded concerns for wildlife but also to the embryonic Progressive movement that would later split the Republican Party under the banner of a big ungulate, a bull moose.

This complex crosscurrent of continental forces becomes personified in the character of Gifford Pinchot, who was every bit as patrician and elitist as Roosevelt. The two men also shared a messianic zeal and scrupulous codes of ethics. Both despised corruption, but while Roosevelt's mission played across the range of national and international issues, especially imperialism, Pinchot cared most about forests. Further, Pinchot worked with a cool, clever, and quiet manipulation of power as opposed to Roosevelt's bombast.

Pinchot used his power and the enabling legislation of the Reclamation Act to amass forest reserves. They were not, however, reserves in the sense of parks. Pinchot was initially a "scientific" forester, trained first at Yale, then later in heavily managed forests in France, Germany, and Switzerland. He believed in logging but in a sustained sort of logging that amounts to, in this school of thought, an intervention in nature that makes nature better and, further, builds pious, stable communities of solid citizens. All of this work was to be managed, overseen, and husbanded by Pinchot himself.

To do this, Pinchot engineered a seemingly innocuous bureaucratic move that resonates to this day and has resulted in perhaps the biggest structural hurdle to true conservation on American public lands. It is the one move that still leaves us with a structure of government conservation that defies logic and reform, owing to a schizophrenic approach to public lands. At the time, the Bureau of Forests was within the Department of the Interior, the same department that controlled the disposition of public lands, which were held for settlement; those that remained unclaimed were in limbo. Pinchot saw the forest reserves as having been withdrawn from this in-limbo status. They were now in use, preserving water for irrigation and providing a steady supply of timber. Therefore, forestry looked something like timber farming, so forested land should not fall within the jurisdiction of the Interior but, rather, be placed within the Department of Agriculture.

Pinchot was playing practical politics. The system of reserves was heavily opposed by Western boomers, loggers, miners, and even ranchers. Pinchot's moving the reserves to the Department of Agriculture was a way to split off the ranchers from this coalition. His forest service would monitor grazing rights on those reserves, meaning ranchers would get access to the forests; they still had no legal access to all other public lands. Pinchot enticed the ranchers with the first legally recognized reserve for grazing. The scheme worked, and Pinchot got his way.

Meanwhile, all of this maneuvering applied only to forested lands. (Pinchot, however, did have a terribly liberal definition of "forest." Congressmen at the time wondered aloud when he would extend forest protection to the entire surface of the Great Salt Lake.) On the plains, the unforested public lands not yet claimed by homesteaders remained in limbo. The cattlemen by then were lobbying heavily for legislation to include those lands in a commons composed of federal grazing lands much like those in Pinchot's forests, but the notion of conservation had not yet evolved to the point that it extended protection to any plot that could be plowed.

In the meantime, Pinchot's maneuverings triggered a head-on confrontation with Congress, which exploded in February 1907, when Congress passed a bill forbidding Pinchot to designate any more of the public domain as forest. The bill hit Roosevelt's desk, and he left it sitting there unsigned while he and Pinchot literally huddled over maps. The two drove clerks in twenty-four-hour shifts until they could draft orders creating twenty-one new forest reserves and enlarging eleven already-existing reserves in six western states. Only then did Roosevelt sign the bill, which his executive orders had now rendered meaningless.

To assert that Roosevelt's conservation was then simply utilitarianism is too simplistic; any blanket assertion falls way short of describing such a complex and enigmatic presidential mind. In 1903, he visited both Yellowstone and Yosemite national parks. At both he behaved in ways that signaled a profound commitment to the wilds. In Yellowstone, he simply disappeared for a long period, eluding his entourage so that he could bask in solitude. He spent his time in Yosemite with John Muir, the living antithesis of Gifford Pinchot, then ended his visit by banning commerce in a small portion of Yosemite, creating the right of a landscape to exist for its own sake. Yosemite was, even then, plagued by commercialism. Later, he told Californians that such places must be preserved, in Muir's sense of the word, not Pinchot's. "We are not building this country of ours for a day. It is to last through the ages."[8]

Roosevelt's mind was bending toward a serious departure from our past and our relationship with public lands. He derived his new view directly from his personal relationship with wild lands. The departure was a direct contradiction of Jefferson, whom he despised. Democracy, he asserted, did not rest solely on freeholders and private property. His belief first became explicit in a message he delivered after visiting Yellowstone, which was then a preserve for bison as a result of his and his elitist friends' direct action.

> Every man who appreciates the majesty and the beauty of the wilderness and of wild life, should strike hands with the far-sighted men who wish to preserve our material resources, in the effort to keep our forests and our game-beasts, game-birds, and game-fish—indeed all the living creatures of prairie and woodlands and seashore—from wanton destruction. Above all, we should recognize that the effort toward this end is essentially a democratic movement. It is entirely within our power as a nation to preserve large tracts of wilderness, which are valueless for agricultural purposes and unfit for settlement, as playgrounds for rich and poor alike.[9]

His row with Congress four years later returned to this theme. From the beginning, it was clear that Roosevelt's singular genius was in circumventing the power structure, the bosses, and the vested interests by pleading his cases directly to the people. He ruled and won by virtue of unprecedented popular support. Pinchot urged him to spend that political currency by taking the forest reserve issue directly to the people, which he did.

As he had from the beginning, Roosevelt presented that issue in terms of water. He was by then under the direct influence of W. J. McGee, one of our first environmental scholars, who believed the environment involves a series of relationships among connected parts, and the whole is connected by water. After a trip on the Mississippi with McGee in 1907, Roosevelt announced that he would convene a national conference on conservation, the first such conference in any nation. He was not simply displaying Rooseveltian bombast when he called it one of the greatest conferences in history; its worth became apparent at the conference itself in May 1908.

When the gathering convened, it included 360 people—all available cabinet members, all nine Supreme Court justices, all of the nation's state and territorial governors, a full complement of congressmen, and representatives of sixty-eight professional societies. It was the birth of the conservation movement in the United States, but the infant was received directly into a family that formed the brewing Progressive movement, which, says one of Roosevelt's biographers, moved from lowercase to capital *P* status during Roosevelt's administration. The public lands historian Louise Peffer writes, "The Conservation Movement was the result [of the conference]. What had actually been a policy, progressively developed, from the opening of Roosevelt's presidency, was now elevated to the position of national crusade by means of Roosevelt's showmanship." [10]

Even at the founding of the movement, the great dichotomy between materialism and ethics was present, as Roosevelt himself explicitly referenced in his remarks convening the meeting. "It [conservation] is the chief material question that confronts us, second—and second always—to the great fundamental questions of morality."[11] Long before Aldo Leopold spelled out his land ethic, Theodore Roosevelt had enunciated his and had explicitly attempted to make it a national ethic.

A footnote to all of this leads us back to the plains, to real events on the Missouri Breaks that soon enough would create the nation's worst environmental catastrophe. A singular presence at Roosevelt's conference warned that our notion of conservation still had some evolving to do. Besides the elected officials and dignitaries ranging from the flinty capitalist Andrew Carnegie to the firebrand populist William Jennings Bryan, the conference hosted an unexpected attendee, James J. Hill, who disliked Roosevelt. Hill was a man the plains knew well. To their largely Scandinavian settlers, he was simply "Yem." Hill's definition of the topic at hand contained no ambiguity. He once said, "Conservation should mean the saving of our resources for future use by providing an economic, scientific and self-perpetuating present use of them. The locking up of resources indefinitely, the exclusion of the people from those natural sources of wealth to which they have a right of access, is not Conservation."[12]

Six

NOTHING CAME UP THAT YEAR

Population without the prairie is a mob, and the prairie without population is a desert.

　　　—*James Hill*

A flaw in the idea of Manifest Destiny created oligarchy. The plan of the expansionists was to send an ever-westward march of yeomen to establish farms, picket fences, churches, and Masonic lodges one hop at a time. This is also our minds' picture of events today, which ignores the fact that the very last places to be settled were stretches of the Great Plains a thousand miles from the Pacific coast, which had by then been settled by Americans for more than a century and had been well known to Europeans for more than three. America is a bicoastal nation with a mostly forgotten center. Our energy, our money, and our people cluster on two coasts. Our frontier is not the West but the center.

　　In the mid-nineteenth century, the problem of maintaining the European claim on Northern California was largely one of transportation. The early toehold gained by fur trappers and gold miners before midcentury could be maintained only by a long ship voyage around South America or, later, by two legs of voyage joined by a quick overland ride across the Isthmus of Panama. A high-value commodity like gold justified such cumbersome transportation, but as the settlers diversified to lumber, canned salmon, cattle, and manufacture along the Pacific coast, commerce needed a shorter link.

In the East and the Midwest, railroads were accustomed to expanding a spur at a time, the short hop over to the next village. With each hop came a bit of extra trade to justify the move. A continental-scale leap such as the one required to leapfrog the plains was unheard of, particularly when snaking over the Rocky Mountains was thrown into the bargain. The solution, proffered by the Lincoln administration, was railroad land grants, large gifts of land to induce the railroads to bridge the enormous gap. In the northern Rockies and in the Cascades, those lands held enough timber to be almost immediately exploited, first for railroad ties, then for the export of timber. For much of the land, though, the only possible payoff would be from farming it, and for that to happen, the railroads needed to recruit farmers and sell the granted land to them.

The railroads initially mounted an effort to recruit settlers to Oregon, not to the plains. Oregon had fertile valleys and temperate conditions similar to those of the East. That is, farmers could have prospered there, but those campaigns mostly failed. Later efforts by the railroads in the 1870s and '80s targeted the more arid lands crossed by the Union Pacific, Northern Pacific, Burlington, and Santa Fe. Paradoxically, those promotions succeeded. The historian Richard White says: "Promotion had become more sophisticated. Railroads quickly discovered the utility of cultivating small-town press. Railroads sponsored free excursions by reporters into the West to view their lands. Having been abundantly liquored and extravagantly fed, reporters were hardly likely to be very critical of lands their hosts wanted them to promote. The stories about western lands that reporters and editors churned out on their return home were usually little more than advertisements for the railroads."[1]

Of course, the government knew this was happening, even though federal officials were then on record as understanding that much of the West was unfit for settlement. Nonetheless, the government viewed population growth anywhere as progress, as economic strength to hold control of the continent, so the government became complicit, so much so that the railroads' excesses extended well beyond hoodwinking settlers. The railroads of the day involved the entire nation in what were not much more than elaborate con games. For instance, several sold stock to pay highly inflated construction costs, then let those construction contracts to dummy companies owned by railroad officers. Chicanery like this produced a series of collapses and nationwide financial panics in the latter half of the century, demonstrating nothing so much as the nation's enormous dependence on the railroads to accomplish its expansion. It wasn't until Theodore Roosevelt's administration, as we have seen, that a president finally asserted that this pattern, especially the stranglehold on western lands, set the railroaders up as oligarchs.

Those of us who in hindsight understand the great tragedy this would foster on the northern plains, in Montana, especially in the Missouri Breaks, usually vilify a particular railroad baron, James J. Hill. He was, after all, the owner of the Great Northern, which in the 1880s extended from Minneapolis and St. Paul west across the plains and Rockies, then to the Pacific coast. Hill's influence has left an indelible mark, even in our language, in that the little towns across northern Montana—Malta, Glasgow, Havre—were named by Hill's agents, who picked them from a map of Europe. All Montanans know the northern tier of towns that stretch parallel to the Canadian border as "the Hi-Line," which derives from the railroad that strung them in a literal line. The center is Havre, still a railroad town and the county seat of Hill County, named for the patriarch. The Amtrak passenger train that still runs the Hi-Line (surviving only because of federal subsidy, the same enabler of all activity along the Hi-Line) is today called, without intended irony, the "Empire Builder." His legacy indeed establishes Hill as a railroad baron, but he shouldn't be sorted into the same bin as the rest of them; he was a very different kind of man.

Hill, born in Canada, migrated, mostly on foot, across the upper Great Lakes states, until he arrived at St. Paul in the late 1850s and took a job as a freight clerk for goods shipped on the Mississippi River.

At that time he was in the fur trade, which was then being carried out by Metis people, as it would be later in the Missouri Breaks. The young clerk reported in 1870, for instance, that Red River carts creaked into his shop freighting 225 bales of buffalo robes containing 2,225 skins worth $230,000.[2] Hill at one point served as a sort of territorial representative who personally negotiated with Louis Riel, the notorious Metis leader who fomented the rebellion that ended in the Metis exodus into Montana.

In his travels into the Red River Valley, the area northwest of St. Paul, he began considering settlement, how a railroad might make settlement possible, and, finally, how he might begin shipping wheat. He started the necessary railroad as well as a relationship with farmers and farming, and this became the core of his business.

The nation's other major rail lines, by then expanding rapidly on their land grants, could make a go of it simply by selling land to farmers; it didn't matter what happened to the farmers. Hill had to approach the matter differently, simply because his railroad had no land grants: "I urged upon the stockholders . . . that the interests of the railroad and the interests of the farmer were identical. . . . The prosperity of the farmer is necessary to our prosperity, and our work of peopling the new country served by our lines would be greatly retarded unless the farmers were able to make a fair living."[3] He later added, "I know that in the first instance my great interest in the agricultural growth of the Northwest was purely selfish. If the farmer was not prosperous, we were poor, and I know what it is to be poor."[4]

He acted accordingly. For instance, when crop losses began plaguing Red River Valley wheat farmers, Hill personally intervened, sending envoys to Russia to seek out better varieties of wheat. When wheat surpluses drove down prices, he mounted a campaign urging farmers to feed the wheat to livestock. He bought a farm of his own, ran agricultural experiments, raised purebred bulls, and gave them away to farmers along his lines to improve their stock. When he found out that a business associate, a Jew, was helping people escape from the anti-Semitic pogroms of Russia, Hill provided land and built forty houses for those refugees.

All of this made for a very different operation from that of most railroad barons by the time his venture had evolved to the Great Northern and began the push west. First, Hill would make that push without outright land grants, but he did need some government intervention. Accordingly, he kept close ties with President Grover Cleveland to ensure passage of the Dawes Act, which deprived the Blackfeet of most of their lands, clearing the way for his railroad. Still, this gave him no land to sell to farmers, so he had to plant successful farmers.

The second difference was that, by all indications, Hill's railroad was run as a sound business. He was an upright Victorian businessman, so much so that when the panics hit the other ventures, he not only survived but was financially strong enough to buy his busted rival, the Northern Pacific. Thus, by the end of the Roosevelt administration, in 1909, the Great Northern had evolved into a solid rock with an honest reputation, the very sort of operation that could precipitate a disaster. The cynical pitch of a con man can inveigle a few of the gullible, but the sincere pleadings of an earnest man can deceive beyond redemption.

In 1902, the empire builder stepped off his train in Malta to do as he often did, to issue a charge to the local reporter. The *Malta Enterprise* quoted James J. Hill: "Tell of the wonders of the Milk River Valley. Greatest Country on earth. Stupendous development. Goodbye."[5] He was addressing a town clearly in transition, but the stupendous development was still a good ten years off. During the 1890s, the big ranches—those of Kohrs, Coburn, Sieben, Phillips—had filled fifteen hundred to two thousand of Jim Hill's railroad cars with cattle every year, a shipment of about a quarter of a million head. By 1908, the *Enterprise* would run an editorial headlined "The Last of the 200,000": "The Range, a stockmen's paradise, is now practically deserted. Within a few miles of Malta a bunch of cattle have been held waiting for shipment to eastern markets. In the eyes of the tenderfoot it is a great big bunch of cattle, but to the old timer who has seen the Malta range covered with cattle thick as ants in a hill, it is the last stand of the greatest industry Montana ever had. Today a shipment will be made, but it is a mere bagatelle to that of ten years ago."[6]

In 1906, John Survant and Robert Coburn went to Argentina looking for better range. The other ranchers either converted to sheep or followed the very strategy John Wesley Powell had forecast: settling along river bottoms. Recall that the first decade of the century brought irrigation to the Milk River Valley, and those early-day cowmen were among the first to claim or buy up that land. What little bit of irrigated land there was quickly went to supporting a new sort of ranching that would replace the open range. Ranchers used the water to raise a new crop that was all the rage, alfalfa, which was cut and bundled as hay to feed cattle during the long plains winters. Ranching had become the hybrid of farming and herding that it remains to this day. From the outset, it depended on the irrigation projects from Theodore Roosevelt's Reclamation Act.

Meanwhile, the nature of the open range shifted dramatically when the sheep industry exploded; the town of Malta alone saw as many as one hundred thousand head show up each spring for shearing. This explosion resulted not only in conflicts between sheepmen and cowmen, which have become one of the most venerated chestnuts of western legend, but also in conflicts between farmers and ranchers, which extend back at least as far as Cain and Abel. The fight was over unsettled public lands, homesteaded lands, and, above all, water. Diehard graziers hated the new barbed wire, especially when it enclosed public lands, as it has done from the start, so they simply cut fences. Gunplay ensued. Court battles erupted.

Regardless of which path was taken, the result was still an overgrazed public domain; successful landownership (that is to say, successful settlement) required river-bottom land and irrigated land, both of which were in short supply. Most of the good land had been either claimed or bought before 1910.

Irrigation triggered a period of manic experimentation in the area. Today, the agricultural land around the Missouri Breaks raises, almost without exception, wheat and hay for cattle. These crops alone have the potential to survive this tough landscape, and even these frequently fail. Yet in the first decade of the century, farmers were bragging about growing everything from pumpkins to flowers. There was talk of a creamery for the benefit of those with dairy herds. Stranger still, most of the boosterism was directed toward corn and hogs, a combination that works only in far wetter and warmer places, such as Iowa. It takes at least forty inches of rain a year to grow corn; the Breaks get ten. No sane northern plainsman today would dream of betting the farm on corn, yet the *Enterprise*, in almost every single issue between 1910 and 1920, printed instructions on raising hogs and corn.

All of this nonsense, though, pales in comparison to the great scam that was to come. Toward the end of the 1910s, the Great Northern Railway mounted an exhibit at its St. Paul station, displaying pumpkins, corn, and sheaves of grain along with photographs of fat cattle and fine horses, all from the Milk River Valley. The railroad was exhibiting the fruits of irrigation in an arid country that had virtually no irrigation left. No matter. Jim Hill had a vision, a sincere and honest plan to deal with all this. He believed in a sort of magic that would wring water from dry soil. For the thousands who would join him in this belief, it would be the mistake of a lifetime, but Jim Hill died a rich man.

⤳

The trail to western settlement was staked with all sorts of hydrophilic lunacy from the beginning. The most quoted is the prominent theory that "rain follows the plow"; that is, the very act of tilling the landscape allegedly produced more rainfall, an article of faith of the mid-nineteenth century. The actual plains experience quickly forced some revision, so by 1890 a more subtle rationalization obtained. The year before, J. R. Dodge, a federal Department of Agriculture statistician, recorded this:

> The settler gradually moved westward and utterly regardless of this dictum [that the West was too arid for the plow] passed the desert line, building his cabin and turning the soil and growing corn, stopping not even at the Colorado line; and today he is growing a better crop of maize than is the farmer in Michigan or northern New York. He has been told that a year of drought and starvation would come and some pinching droughts have confronted him, as they have the farmer of Illinois; still he has pushed westward with heroic determination, plowing and subduing the soil and showing by his improvements that he is there to stay. What is the cause of this magical change?

> *Some High-Powered Deductions on Meteorology*

> As the mines in which the ores have been hidden for ages have been discovered, so a new agricultural country that has also existed for ages has been discovered by light of practical experience and a higher science. Has there been an increase in rainfall? The records of the rain gauge do not show it very conclusively, though it is now said that this instrument is no true test of real precipitation. Yet there is a change of climate. The agricultural values of the climate have increased. The moisture that was before carried away, flowing from the surface line like water from a duck's back, is held in the soil, taken up by the roots of plants, given out through their leaves, or evaporated from the surface of the soil and a marked increase of humidity of the atmosphere is the result, which is shown in the dews unknown before. This humidity is a factor in plant growth though it is not made apparent by such a measure of precipitation as the rain gauge.[7]

Twisted and selfish government rationalizations about climate change are not a twenty-first-century invention. Dodge's line of thought was further refined through the good offices of James J. Hill. Hill had in his employ Hardy Campbell, not a flimflam man, but a respected crop scientist of the day, a North Dakota farmer who developed a system of dryland farming there. The system came to bear his name, and he used Hill's backing to trumpet its virtues. Campbell recommended a regime of plowing, of summer fallow in alternate years, and a relatively diverse system of crop rotation with wheat at its center. Wrote Campbell, "Recent investigations of dry farming, or farming without irrigation, have demonstrated that paying crops can be produced in regions where annual precipitation is as low as ten inches."[8] This claim is considered absurd today; the dividing line between grassland and desert is approximately ten inches, which is about the average rainfall of the Missouri Breaks, the very place Jim Hill had in mind for his settlers. Nonetheless, Campbell claimed, "This kind of farming has been practiced for many years, but it is only since 1904 that the system has developed into a profitable industry. Thousands of bushels of wheat, barley and oats are being produced on land that five years ago was thought to be less than worthless."[9] The best measure of Campbell's sincerity is that he himself bought a large dryland farm in Montana and eventually went broke, just as did most who tried his system.

Hill also employed Thomas Shaw, a professor at Minnesota Agricultural College, who provided academic backing to Campbell's system. The railroad spread the tidings of Shaw's forays into the West to observe for himself that dry farms around a town called Homestead had produced abundant crops for a long time, which in his view was defined as two or three years. The West is notorious for never presenting a year that is average. That is, those areas said to have an annual average of fifteen inches of rain typically get ten or three or four in some years, then thirty the next. The winds also bring wild fluctuations in fortune. Campbell and Shaw based their systems on the results of a few good years; they had no time for long-term studies, because the land needed to be settled.

Writes a group of Montana historians, "Hill was very much a Jeffersonian democrat, who believed in rural virtues and saw the family farm as the backbone of American society. He envisioned the fertile plains

of Montana and the Dakotas as the granary of the world, neatly par-
titioned into small family farms."[10] Shaw, Hill, and Campbell magnified their ideas through local booster groups and especially newspapers, not just in the West, but throughout the United States. This
and the Enlarged Homestead Act and a companion, the Desert Lands
Entry Act, which was meant to stimulate irrigation, produced a land
rush pointed toward the string of towns on the Hi-Line beginning
about 1909.

A few made their own way west (the model T Ford was already available), but for most, the vehicle of migration was Hill's own Great
Northern Railway. Typically, the settler left St. Paul by renting a freight
car for fifty dollars, into which he would load the family's furniture,
tools, supplies, enough lumber for a shack, and livestock. The father
and any children who tended the stock in the car could ride free of
charge. Those who didn't do so paid fares in coach cars. The trip took
about five days, after which the settlers were disgorged into one of Jim
Hill's towns, blinking from the darkness of the boxcars into the flash-
ing brilliance of a treeless grassland.

There is money to be made in farming as long as one doesn't farm,
an adage that held then as it does now. Then, the money was going
to locators, men who would meet the cars and, for about twenty dollars, direct the naive to a land claim. They did a land-office business.
The federal land office at Great Falls processed about fifteen hundred
new land claims a month, beginning in 1910. During the first three
months of that year, the Great Northern moved more than a thousand
immigrant cars into Montana. Between 1913 and 1915, five thousand
settlers moved into Phillips County, which today has a population of
just over four thousand.[11]

The plains quickly became a patchwork of 320-acre tracts spread
with as much tilled ground as farmers could handle and dotted with
forlorn little shacks, some of which remain, sagging and rotting, scant
hard evidence now of that way of life. The historian Joseph Kinsey

Howard began his research in the 1940s, so had access to firsthand accounts. He offers a description:

> The shacks usually were one room, about twelve by fourteen feet, with a gable roof, a window in each end, and a door in the middle of the long side. They were set flat on the ground without a foundation, but often had a tiny "cellar" under a trap door in the floor, to serve as a refrigerating compartment. The better houses were clapboarded, but thousands of them merely had tarpaper tacked over the exterior siding; the first strong winds ripped much of it off.
>
> Old newspapers, especially rotogravure sections, were pasted up for wall covering. A sagging bed, stools, a table made of boxes, and curtained shelves for cupboards made up the furniture.[12]

Such descriptions conjure a vision of people without options, the destitute, illiterate, peasant immigrants desperate enough to face these conditions. This, however, was not true, either on the northern plains or in the West in general. In the four-state area of Montana, Wyoming, South Dakota, and Colorado, only 20–30 percent of the settlers were immigrants, and many of them were well-educated Germans and Scandinavians. More revealing, most of the settlers, native-born and immigrant alike, had never farmed before. A survey of fifty-eight farmers in a township in Montana found that only twenty-three had prior farming experience. That same group included two schoolteachers, three "Maiden Ladies," six musicians, two wrestlers, and a "World Rover."[13] The settlers tended to be young and, more important, overwhelmingly literate, a revealing characteristic.

Looking back on this doomed wave of settlement, we are tempted to lay blame on a lack of information. Who would brave a Montana winter in a one-room tarpaper shack if she (a surprisingly large proportion of the settlers, maybe 20 percent, were single women) knew anything at all about a Montana winter? But that's not quite the problem. In fact, the settlers had an amazingly large body of information;

it was just bad information. And this was not solely the doing of rail-road flimflam men and their pet reporters. "Scientific" agriculture was being born, and every single new quack method and measure was faith-fully reprinted by local newspapers and spread far and wide in such tracts as agriculture department pamphlets. The U.S. Department of Agriculture, the state's Agricultural Research Station, and Montana State College—the state's land-grant school—were all actively pros-elytizing to the settlers. In a sense, the dryland-farming settlement boom was brought on by an information age, a time when the pow-erful were gaining control over the dissemination of information to an audience not yet cured of its gullibility. Imagine an industry pro-pelled by bloggers. Significantly, Hill's money backed more than just railroads; he was also a major investor in the *New York Times*. This his-tory places the present and widespread distrust of government among surviving ranchers in a new light. A process of cultural selection left in place only those who did distrust outside advice, especially that of the government. This selection pressure was to be reapplied many times between then and now.

A central theme in that initial barrage was advice to "farm big." The first such piece of advice came in the form of prescribing big hitches, involving teams of as many as twenty horses pulling massive plows, but this almost immediately gave way to proselytizing for mechanized tillage. The April 27, 1911, edition of the *Malta Enterprise* reported that the Great Northern train had chugged into town bearing some-thing more momentous than the usual load of immigrant wagons. One E.J. Gunnison was about to take delivery on a new gasoline-powered Avery tractor. Gunnison, who reportedly did not like horses, was quoted: "I'll get something that will be worth more than a dozen horses and keep it on a good gasoline diet instead of expensive feed three times a day. I'll put it under cover three or four months of the year and it won't eat its head off while resting."

This dictum was more or less officially adopted by the various or-gans of scientific farming, which were very quickly urging all settlers to farm big with tractors. The paragon of the period in Montana was Thomas D. Campbell, who, with the backing of J. P. Morgan, put together a wheat farm of 150,000 acres with 500 plows, 600 seed drills, 72 binders, and 32 combines and threshers. Present-day farmers who survived the crisis of the 1980s know well the next bit of advice, the same bit that precipitated that recent crisis. The settlers, having been told to farm big, quickly heard the corollary: that mechanized farming is capital intensive, so farming big means borrowing big. What, after all, was a mortgage bearing single-digit interest when the scientific information of the day was soberly advising settlers to expect returns of 25 percent on their investment? The literate settlers read this and signed on dotted lines. What their government said in writing had to be true.

Fueling this was a wheat boom, largely brought on by World War I, with its high demand for wheat, coupled with an above-average rainfall that boosted production, not just around Malta, but throughout the northern plains. Regionwide, farmers plowed up an additional five million acres of virgin short-grass prairie during the war. The total value of farm machinery in the region increased 240 percent between 1900 and 1920. Single farms reported clear annual profits of seventy-five thousand dollars shortly after the war.[14]

In less than a decade this news made its way around the country, in fact, into Europe. Any railroad recruiting was by now superfluous. Profits fueled a sort of wheat rush that was not at all the settlement envisioned by Thomas Jefferson and those who passed the Homestead Act of 1862. Many of the new settlers were out to cash in and move on in the fashion of gold miners, not farmers. The period, along with the inhospitable conditions of the plains, brought a new term into agronomy: the *suitcase farmer*. These people claimed a piece of land, bought or hired the tractors to plow it in the spring, moved back into town or to a city far away for the summer, returned in the fall to hire threshers, then relocated to a more pleasant climate to avoid the brutal plains winter. Monocrop wheat agriculture and machinery allow this sort of loose tenancy, a pattern that is still familiar to Montana's wheat farmers, many of whom head south to Arizona or New Mexico to ride out the winter.

This is no small matter but in fact set the social pattern that prevails throughout the high plains to this day. There may have been something to Jefferson's vision of local democracy, steepled churches, and white-picket-fenced communities with deep roots to the land and kinship, but no such pattern could emerge from capital-intensive suitcase farming. Howard, besides being a historian, spent a good deal of his career working with progressive experiments designed to bolster the integrity of individual communities. He knew the value of a small town's social fabric and was familiar with the towns of eastern Montana of the mid-twentieth century. He wrote:

> In the east and middle west and in the better-settled Pacific Coast states there exist hundreds of "cultural communities"—groups of neighborhoods about a central medium-sized city. These fulfill the cultural needs of residents of that section, and through education, entertainment and the building up through generations of an intangible but stalwart community loyalty, they tend to hold people within their borders.
>
> Such communities have no counterparts in Montana. The few cities are scores of miles apart, and none of them has a surrounding group of rural communities. The rural towns, with some exceptions, have a deadly sameness and frequently consist of nothing but a grain elevator or two, a general store, a saloon, a church, and a handful of nondescript houses.[15]

In the early twenty-first century, the description remains apt, with a few possible additions: "an *abandoned* grain elevator or two, a *convenience* store, a saloon, a *Bible-thumper fundamentalist* church, and a handful of nondescript house *trailers*." Today there are even fewer of these small rural towns.

❧

Tough, inhuman towns can hang on, but gross violations of nature's design tend to be rather quickly punished. The exceptional rainfall pattern of the 1910s collapsed, bringing drought, a familiar pattern to the plains but one new to the freshly arrived farmers. Virgin soils and abundant moisture had combined to give Montana an average yield of twenty-five bushels of wheat to the acre between 1900 and 1916. Three years after this period, the drought hit. Hill County, for instance, recorded a total of four inches of rain in all of 1919. Yields fell to two bushels per acre, one-tenth that of the wartime years. Meanwhile, the war boom wound down, and so did wheat prices, falling by more than 50 percent. In Montana alone in 1919, the combination of drought and price decreases resulted in a fifty-million-dollar loss. Most of the farmers were wiped out that year, which is one of the reasons we have no solid measure of the scale of the boom. Many had come after the 1910 census and then were already gone before the full increase could be officially measured in the count of 1920.

Half of Montana's remaining farmers lost their land to mortgage foreclosure between 1921 and 1925. Those who could afford a ticket out on Jim Hill's railroad quit the country, but many simply became destitute. Hill County reported three thousand indigents in 1919, in an era before government-paid welfare.[16] The Red Cross was then the only recourse, and it was overwhelmed.

This drought, though, was not a natural disaster but rather a normal occurrence on the plains. Left to its own devices, a short-grass prairie simply rolls with this punch. Some animals die, but the mostly nomadic species of the plains move a few hundred miles to locate better conditions—under normal circumstances, that is. But those five million acres of freshly plowed land, plus everything that had been plowed or overgrazed earlier, had been stripped of their survival gear, the co-evolved species that allow the land to recover. The tough circumstances of the Dirty Thirties actually began on the northern plains in 1919. A few wet years in the early 1920s provided some small respite to the

few farmers who had held on after the bust of 1919, but drought began again in earnest in the late '20s with a far more powerful punch.

Gladys Miller, the Phillips County resident who wrote a WPA history of her place, summarized the period:

> 1927 and another bumper crop [of wheat]. Prices were low, and around
> us many of our neighbors had sold off their cattle and other livestock.
> They traded for cars, for machinery, for furniture, for anything they
> needed in order to put in more wheat and farm on a still larger scale.
> A few of the [former] Iowa and Dakota farmers stuck stubbornly to
> livestock. The range was covered with horses, which were for the most
> part unclaimed. It had become far easier "to crank up little Henry
> [Ford]" said one farmer recently than to "spend an entire morning
> rounding up a bunch of snakey broncs. I could buzz around a lot faster
> too. I went to work at three A.M. and didn't come in until dark during
> spring's work and just turned the milch cows out on the range 'till fall.
> I wanted to bust more sod, pick up more rocks, and get the larger price
> so I didn't care about my cattle."

The grain prices continued to go down in spite of drought. Banks
were failing. Credit harder to obtain. The grass on the range began to
dry up early in June of 1928. 1929 drier still. "We had about forty pigs
in addition to my other livestock that fall. Our sixty acres of barley produced about thirty bushels in all when combined. Needless to say, the
poor pigs went hungry until we could get rid of them at whatever the
buyer wanted to pay."

Great cracks began to appear in the prairie sod. That year the writer
taught school at the Dunbar ranch. I lived in the school house with my
little daughter. In April of 1930 the wind began to blow at four o'clock.
In a few minutes it became so dark I lighted our lamp. At first I paid
little attention, but by seven the roar of the wind and the swaying of
the western wall of the school house alarmed me. I opened the door
on the north, thinking to run to the ranch about one-half mile away.
The blinding force of the wind, the sting of the dust and gravel forced
me back. The roar increased and the dust in the room made it hard to
breathe. I took my little daughter and crawled under the desk. The
school house stood on eight cement blocks so I expected every mo-

ment to have it topple over. Some piece of machinery banged against the west side of the building. I heard something bump and bang over the ground; it seemed to be some buildings. But the blackness was so dense I could see nothing. We crouched under the desk all night, and I exhausted my repertoire of songs and stories in order to keep Miss Seven Year Old from worrying. Morning and things looked a little better, but no children came to school that day as the dust and gravel would blind them. The storm died away about 5 P.M. and I went out to take toll of the damage. All the outbuildings in the School yard were blown about one-quarter mile down in the field and were wrecked. Mr. Dunbar's oats planted on about 100 acres of summer fallow a few days before lay in great drifts of dust and seed like snow drifts.

Nothing came up that year. In the summer Mr. Dunbar and his men stacked Russian thistles for feed for the sheep.[17]

Seven

PAVING THE ROAD TO HELL

Years will come of abundance and years will come of disaster, and between the two the people will be prosperous and unprosperous.

—*John Wesley Powell*

Analyzing the causes of the present disaster, the committee assigned primary importance to the attempt, which has been made for several decades to impose on the Great Plains a system of agriculture not adapted to the region. . . . On the western Plains, it was both a stimulus to over-cultivation and a condemnation of the cultivators to poverty.

—*Secretary of Agriculture Henry A. Wallace, 1937*

The spring of 1932 was bad enough, with fourteen regional dust storms, but 1933 brought a total of thirty-eight severe storms, one of which blew dust off high plains farms all the way to New York City. Nothing, however, equaled the fury of 1934, nothing before or since. The spring winds that year pried 350 million tons of topsoil from over-plowed and overgrazed drought-stricken fields of Montana, Wyoming, Nebraska, and the Dakotas in three days. Chicago's surface area gathered four pounds of dust per capita. Washington DC's days turned dark. Boston, New York City, and ships in the Atlantic were coated with plains states' real estate.

The following spring, the dust flew once again, but in part with a different result. Franklin Roosevelt's administration was then proposing legislation to conserve soil on the plains, but the bill was stuck in Con-

gress. Hugh Bennett, the New Dealer who was to head the Soil Conservation Service that this legislation would create, was scheduled to
testify before Congress in support of the bill, but he deliberately de-
layed his appearance. Bennett knew that a more effective witness was
headed in from the Southwest. A dust storm was under way in New
Mexico, and when its proceeds reached Washington DC on April 19,
Bennett finally appeared before Congress, pointed to the dust-darkened
skies outside, and said, "This, gentlemen, is what I am talking about."
Would that nature could consistently lobby so effectively on its own
behalf. The bill passed.

Not that the New Deal lacked effective conventional lobbyists.
FDR's administration stood in stark contrast to any before and most
since in its use of a brain trust, a cast of colorful and powerful characters who battled very publicly, both with Congress and with one
another, for the most ambitious social agenda in the nation's history.
It had to be ambitious. Panics and financial failures had occurred before, but none was like this one, rooted deeply in failed policy and
environmental disaster. The economy had collapsed, but that was no
longer the principal issue. The real specter was the collapse of the
nation itself.

The story of Theodore Roosevelt's administration can indeed be
told through character, but no doubt it must be through the character of TR himself, with perhaps a bit of Gifford Pinchot thrown in as
a foil. The story of FDR's reign, however, can be cast only in plural
characters: Henry Wallace, a Progressive to the core, controversial
even then, vice president, later a presidential candidate, whose views
today would, if not lead to his imprisonment, at least render him a
political pariah; Harold Ickes, secretary of the interior, the man who,
as a subsequent chapter will argue, created conservation as we know it;
Rexford Tugwell, Rex the Red, as the press knew him; Bernard Baruch;
Cordell Hull; Henry Morgenthau; Bob Marshall, father of wilderness;
Lorena Hickock, journalist and a special friend to Eleanor Roosevelt;
Eleanor herself—in the end, literally hundreds of smart Progressives,

each an active character in his or her own right. Their interactions made for both a complex weave that would face down a serious threat of global fascism and a host of accomplishments that remain a part of the nation's social fabric today. The embedded story of public lands, land use, and agriculture stands as a signal accomplishment, as does, ultimately, the current farm welfare state. This, too, can be told through character, that of two men, both Montanans. The first, M. L. Wilson, a failed dry farmer, was an obscure thoughtful man with an idea, a county extension agent whose name would become famous and be both honored and cursed at the highest levels of FDR's administration. His small idea took root in the niche of catastrophe that was created in and eventually spread through the West to become the basis of what is today the region's most serious land-use problem. The second, Henry Lantz, the county extension agent of Phillips County, stationed in Malta, was the character who devised a program that serves to make the case that today's farm and ranch welfare state began dead center in the Missouri Breaks. Lantz meant no harm with his actions, at least as far as I know, but any certainty is impossible because he is mostly forgotten today.

Depopulation is simply another abstraction trapped in numbers until it manifests itself in a community's stories. When that happens, one realizes that people who leave are of a certain type, and they take their stories—and therefore the stories of that type—with them. Whole families and, along with them, whole threads of history, ideas, can all disappear without a trace. The people of the plains who survived the droughts of the 1920s and the ensuing Dust Bowl years tended to be of a type: They were the people who had preceded the wave of railroad-recruited settlement in the 1910s. They had come earlier, had learned some hard lessons in ranching, had claimed the best river-bottom lands, learned to irrigate, and developed the hybrid between ranching and farming that remains today in the Breaks.

The newcomers, literate, educated people of dreams, were a different sort. We know this, for instance, by comparing the political culture of today, the rock-ribbed, know-nothing conservatism of red-state America, with the politics of the time, which was simply red. The Dust Bowl years radicalized the plains, and left-of-center socialist movements thrived. The Nonpartisan League and, after it, the Farmer-Labor Party (FLP) both spread from Minnesota westward as Progressive third-party movements. The latter party remains today in Minnesota as the DFL (the Democratic-Farmer-Labor Party) but has vanished without a trace in North Dakota and Montana.

More telling was the case of Sheridan County and the town of Plentywood, Montana, just east of the Missouri Breaks. From just after World War I until the mid-1930s, American Communists nationwide had three choices of reading material: the *Communist*, the *Daily Worker*, and the *Producers News*. The first two were, of course, published in New York City; the last, in Plentywood by the radical Charles E. Taylor. His paper was the West's mouthpiece for the Communist Party, as well as for the Nonpartisan League and the FLP. The Communist Party of the United States was a regular advertiser.[1]

Taylor, who by 1922 had become a card-carrying Communist, ran for and was elected to the state senate that year. Two other party members, Clair Stoner and Rodney Salisbury, were elected as state representative and sheriff, respectively. The party ran Sheridan County for more than ten years. This was no anomaly laid to the peculiarities of either Taylor's character or Sheridan County. In fact, part of the Roosevelt administration's later urgency to deal with the Dust Bowl's problems was an explicit fear that the radical populism of the northern plains would foment revolution. Roosevelt both feared this and played to it in campaigning for his first election in 1932. During that time, M. L. Wilson, the broke Montana dry farmer who was by then an agricultural scientist and a chief adviser of FDR's, drafted a key speech laying out policies that resulted in Roosevelt's carrying the plains by a wider margin than any other area of the country. In modern terms, the West held the bluest of the blue states. By that time, though, an idea in the head of one of Wilson's protégés, Henry Lantz, the Phillips County extension agent, was well on its way toward reshaping the West.

Lantz is one of those people who left little trace of himself; mostly he gets just the occasional reference in oral histories, extension agent reports, local histories, and high-level accounts of the New Deal. I tracked him through these odd vestigial traces for months and was never able to hang much flesh on the bones of his story. Once, I found an eighty-six-year-old woman in Malta, Betty Ulrich, who actually had worked for Lantz as a secretary during the New Deal. She remembered that when she was a child, Lantz would show up at her parents' ranch periodically and have a look at her 4-H projects. She said, "He was a great big guy, nice, too." Lantz and his wife, she thought, were childless, and she had no idea what became of the man. His story just petered out among the many of Phillips County.

One of Lantz's fleeting mentions on the record occurs in one of Joseph Kinsey Howard's histories. It's the closest the record comes to a characterization: "Raised a Mennonite and conscientious objector, Lantz nevertheless entered the first World War and was in several major engagements. He came out with a lifelong hatred for the regimentation of men's minds and for the occasional arrogance of bureaucracy."[2] Hard to say to what extent that is the projection of Howard's own mind, but it does dovetail with the record. For instance, an oral history from a DC-level bureaucrat mentions an order from the White House to fire Lantz right away for his obstreperousness, an order the bureaucrat slipped into a desk drawer and ignored.[3]

The best evidence I could find of Lantz's project was a rack of tall, narrow, metal file drawers, maybe a dozen drawers in all, each the size of business envelopes stacked on end and crammed with handwritten deeds of homesteaders and ranchers turning their land over to the federal government. Some contain earnest handwritten letters from people claiming to be destitute, which they no doubt were, and, according to the *Phillips County News*, desperately wanting the "$5.00 an acre for all lands that have been cleared of rock and plowed, $3.00 an acre for first-class grazing lands, $2 for second, $1 for third" that the government was offering.[4] (See figure 2.)

Howard's characterization of Lantz and everything else about him on the record tell us he fit with the spirit of the time. He was a Progressive and was comfortable with the swirl of radical politics of the high plains. But more to the point, he was a man of science, as all the agronomists of Montana at that time thought of themselves—a network built and headed by M. L. Wilson. A great deal more flesh is on Wilson's story, and it tells much about the evolution of the New Deal.

Wilson himself was an Iowa farm boy at a fortuitous time, when Iowa was the center of an agricultural revolution. At the center of that revolution was a single family, the Wallaces, the same family that was to produce Henry Wallace, the vice president and agriculture secretary under whom Wilson would serve. Henry A. Wallace's earliest contribution, however, was technical and sufficient to stake a claim on a spot in history books even if so much more had not followed in his life. Long before he entered politics, Wallace fomented his own little revolution with work he started as a high school junior. He was then already established in a farm belt dynasty. He was the third Henry in a line of Henry Wallaces. The senior Henry, Henry A.'s grandfather, was a Presbyterian preacher who left the ministry to serve another flock: Iowa's farmers. He published what evolved into a national agricultural newspaper, *Wallaces' Farmer and Dairyman*, while keeping a hand in the budding Iowa agricultural college and in national Progressive Republican politics. He was simply the most influential voice in agriculture at the time and widely respected. Thus, when a young M. L. Wilson first encountered the elder Wallace, generally known as "Uncle Henry," it was an important moment for him that he still talked about in his retirement.

Wilson's first encounter came when he was a student writer for the agricultural college's newspaper and drew the assignment of inter-

Figure 2. Editorial cartoon from the Phillips County News, *Malta, Montana.*

viewing Uncle Henry. "Uncle Henry Wallace was very distinguished looking and a very friendly person. He was a man who smoked cigars all the time. He wore a long, black Prince Albert coat, and the ashes of these cigars were pretty apt to be on his coat," Wilson said.[5] Later, when Wilson was heavily engaged in experiments in Montana, he went to see Uncle Henry when he was dying. "He was aged. He remembered me, and he wanted to know what I was doing and so on, and I told him something about our experiments in corn in Montana. When I opened up that conversation, he said, 'Hold on here. I want my grandson to come in.'"[6]

Corn meant much to the Wallaces. Henry C., who was Uncle Henry's son and Harry A.'s father, wrote for the paper, became widely influential in Progressive Republican politics, and served as secretary of agriculture under Warren Harding, a man whom he regarded as a blank slate on which he could write progressive agricultural policy, by which he and all the Wallaces meant not just crops but also science, sound education, communities with integrity, picket fences, and steeples. Whereas Henry C. shaped national policy, Henry A. shaped everything that has happened in agriculture worldwide ever since. The trigger of this revolution was hybrid corn, which scientists at Woods Hole Laboratory had developed in the 1910s but which was widely regarded as an impractical lab toy at that time. A teacher gave Henry A. some hybrid seed while he was still in junior high school. He experimented with it during his remaining years in high school and through college and made it practical, leading to the Wallace family's founding of Pioneer Hybrid Seeds. The company still is a dominant player in agriculture. The massive increase in yields dramatically increased farmers' incomes. To this day, people who were children at the time remember a hand-to-mouth existence changing almost overnight to a secure life with a car and the possibility of a college education. Hybrid corn transformed the American South from a feudal backwater into an agricultural power.

Hybrid corn was also a model that would eventually spread worldwide as part of the Green Revolution. But before then, it spread to Mexico directly through Henry A. Wallace, who traveled there on vacation just before taking office as FDR's vice president. He couldn't resist visiting some Mexican farmers, if for no other reason than to practice Spanish, and was appalled by the poverty that was the universal state of rural Mexico. He returned to New York, stomped into the offices of the Rockefeller Foundation, and laid out a forceful case for the foundation to invest in developing-world agriculture. That investment became the Green Revolution, and Rockefeller is still the leading source of money for agricultural research in the developing world.

M. L. Wilson knew Henry A. well, even as a young man. No doubt some of this Progressive dynamism, rooted in Wallace's deep faith in the connection between science and progress, rubbed off. Wilson took that faith to the prairies of Montana. He was, in fact, among the literate and gullible who boarded the railroad's "home seekers'" cars in 1908. His source of information was impeccable: not a railroad PR man, but no less than the director of the Montana State Agricultural Station, who told Wilson that if he came, he "would make more money in two or three years than you would in a lifetime in Nebraska."[7]

Wilson hesitated, but in 1909, when Congress passed the Enlarged Homestead Act, he filed a claim on land near Forsyth. His college education in agriculture, his rearing as a farm boy in Iowa, and his solid contacts in Montana, however, were no match for parched earth. By 1910, Wilson was a broke homesteader, not even surviving to cash in on World War I's boom years. Having failed at farming, he elected to teach it, joined up with the budding agricultural school in Bozeman, and served as a county extension agent. When the farmers around Malta listened to advice to borrow money and farm big, they were listening to Wilson. He was a champion of the big hitch, an assembly of five to as many as ten pairs of horses all pulling a single plow, the precursor to the tractor.

Wilson was a dreamer, a believer that experimentation and information could overcome the harsh prairie conditions. His dreaming, though, was not limited to agriculture. Instead, agriculture and science stood at the core of his ethical system, were means to a greater end. Wilson spelled this out in an interview after he retired. After he lost his farm and went to work for the state, he found time to squeeze in graduate school at the University of Wisconsin at Madison, and he summarized that experience as shaping a pragmatism rooted in ethics:

> In religion in our society today, the religious person is the person who is using science as a tool, who has his system of values and beliefs. He could be an orthodox Christian as far as that's concerned because he [an influential professor] didn't get particularly into the theology of things except to talk a good deal about Christ as a fearless fighter who fought evil and just didn't meditate about it, but drove the money changers out of the temple. Therefore, students in the field of economics and the social sciences who sat around and meditated with their hands in their pockets were really evil—they were really sinners—because they had an obligation to use the scientific knowledge that they were acquiring in the fields of the social sciences and to use this knowledge as a weapon, so to speak, for this fight against the problem of evil as it was defined.[8]

This is the messianic zeal he brought to bear on his job as an agricultural extension agent. He set out to use science to perfect society and, toward that end, founded a series of small, semicooperative farming communities based on irrigated crops. Always he regarded those as experiments in balancing the scale of an operation against cost of capital, prices, and production. These experiments were financial failures, however, largely because of fluctuating prices, so Wilson would later come to the Roosevelt administration with a bedrock belief in farm price supports designed to stop those fluctuations.

Eventually, Wilson began supervising Montana's county extension agents, one of whom was Henry Lantz. He visited Lantz often and remained in contact with him throughout the Depression. There is no way to track the direction of influence between the two men, but given their predispositions, it was more a matter of a meeting of minds than a changing of minds. Lantz was a dreamer, too, but he did his dreaming in an area Wilson never really considered. All his life Wilson was a crop man, concentrating his efforts on wheat and irrigation. Lantz, however, learned his lessons in dry farming in Phillips County, beginning in the 1920s. It was an experience that taught him that the nation had to come to grips with arid lands, grazing, and something more or less unmentioned in a century and a half of political culture devoted to private property: commons. Lantz came to believe in the value of land held in common for the common good.

During the 1920s, national policy was still in denial, the somewhat permanent state of national policy. That is, we have seen how the open-range period forced cattlemen to appropriate federal lands, simply because there was no legal mechanism to enable grazing vast areas. The land was being held until homesteaders might claim it. But by 1920, it was clear that not many homesteaders were claiming it, and most who tried were broke before they proved up their claims. The stock of federal grasslands was not decreasing but increasing. Still, these lands remained in a sort of legal limbo, hostage to the nation's belief in homesteading and the yeoman myth.

Since 1901, the cattlemen had proposed bills allowing grazing rights on federal lands; all were quickly defeated. The situation finally became so acute that, in 1931, Herbert Hoover offered to cede all unoccupied federal lands to the states, the very idea that became the key demand of the right-wing "Sagebrush Rebellion" in the West in the late twentieth century. But in the 1930s the states were wiser, viewing the arid lands as a burden and declining Hoover's offer.

Even before this, though, Congress did authorize an experiment in establishing a grazing commons. In 1926, a group of ranchers and ag experts hatched a scheme for a cooperative grazing district in Montana's Custer County. They lobbied Montana congressman Scott

Leavitt, a Republican, who agreed to a horseback tour of the proposed district. He then lobbied Montana's senior senator, Thomas J. Walsh, and together they steered a special bill through Congress establishing the Mizpah-Pumpkin Creeks Grazing Association experiment, named for the two streams that defined that area. It would allow a cooperative of ranchers to fence public lands, then jointly administer the area themselves as a grazing district. In 1927, Henry Lantz traveled south from Malta, visited the Mizpah-Pumpkin Creeks experiment, then folded that idea in with another that had been percolating in his brain.

Lantz's master plan for the commons hinged on a map. He had done what the artist George Catlin had done before and what a coalition of GIS mappers would do a couple of generations later. He lifted himself up on Catlin's "imaginary wings" and used the vantage to map not the surface but the unseen subsurface of the area. Lantz's plan was based on a "scientific" mapping of Phillips County soils. Simply, he hatched the radical idea that some of those soils were fit for farming, and some were not.

The second element of this idea, which became known as the "Malta plan," keyed on the drive toward irrigation that had begun building during Theodore Roosevelt's administration. Phillips County had indeed obtained its big ditch and its reservoir, which created thousands of acres of irrigable land along the Milk River, but by the time Lantz came along in the 1920s, most of those acres had never been irrigated as planned. Instead, much of the land had been snatched up by speculators, who offered it on the market at the premium price it probably deserved. The wave of settlers, however, were not willing to pay as long as free land was available, and most of their information was telling them that all the money was to be made in dry-farming wheat. So while the worst land filled with settlers, the best lay idle. Lantz, of course, knew this, so his plan was simple enough. The government would buy out the broke homesteaders who had flocked to free dry land only ten or fifteen years before. Next, it would buy the irrigated land along the Milk River, land it had made valuable only twenty years before by subsidizing irrigation. Then it would settle the uprooted homesteaders there on much smaller plots, on the order of forty acres.

As it evolved, though, the Malta plan was more than a land swap. Lantz imagined building planned communities—houses, barns, and all—on the irrigated land, patterned after the farm communities Wilson had experimented with in the 1910s and on into the '20s. Those farmers would be expected to use some of their income to pay back the government for the farms. Until 1932, however, Lantz's idea was nothing more than that. His requests for money to carry out his plan fell on deaf ears during the Hoover administration, which was then content to let the social problems of the plains fall on the Red Cross. The Red Cross was then stretched so thin that it could offer each needy person a food allotment of only ten cents a day. State and local welfare was nonexistent. At least a third of the families still on the plains needed some form of relief by then.

Franklin Roosevelt liked to call himself a farmer, a title he believed he deserved from his management of the family estate in New York. Indeed, when he began running for office, he did so as a farmer, driving around upstate New York to meet at town halls and Grange halls to talk prices with the local potato and dairy farmers. He was, however, no more a farmer than George W. Bush is a rancher. In fact, he was an exceedingly shrewd politician and a smart man, who surrounded himself with people of his kind. When he ran for president in 1932, he quickly realized that Hoover's Depression was deeply rooted in farm-state economics as it existed in the plains.

Early in his campaign, in September 1932, FDR planned a whistle-stop tour through the West and, early in that tour, scheduled what he believed would be a pivotal speech on agricultural policy in Topeka, Kansas. (At the time, September, less than two months before the election, was considered early in the campaign.) In that speech, FDR out-

lined an ambitious program of tariffs, price supports, voluntary measures, and farmers' cooperatives, all designed to address the crisis of
the Midwest and West. But more important, when Roosevelt spoke,
he spoke as a farmer, as someone who sympathized with the people
and understood the problems that had thrown their region into
poverty. The posture was pure Roosevelt, but the policy had been laid
out by M. L. Wilson in a memo to Roosevelt aide Raymond Moley.
The speech, in fact, followed what became known in the administration as the "Wilson outline." A memo from Roosevelt brain truster
Henry Morgenthau to Wilson acknowledges the connections, but
more intriguingly Morgenthau says of that speech, "I will try to supply the missing link on land utilization."[9] The "Land Utilization Program" would later become the official name of the national program
modeled on Henry Lantz's Malta plan.

Wilson himself was not present for the speech in Topeka and probably didn't even hear it, although it was broadcast nationally by radio.
He recalled:

> I had a radio at Bozeman. Bozeman is in the mountains, and the re-
> ception sometimes was not too good. On the 14th, I believe I was on
> one of the Fairway Farms [his experimental farms], more than likely
> up at Poplar, Montana at the Lone Warrior Farm. That's almost at
> the Canadian line, and the spring wheat harvest goes over into Sep-
> tember, particularly when you combine. I don't believe we were com-
> bining, but I think we were up there on some business. I don't think
> we had a radio there that was strong enough to get FDR's speech, so
> that I had to get my first version of the Topeka speech on local news
> reporting comments in the morning paper of the next day, which car-
> ried the whole draft of the speech. I naturally felt pretty good when
> I read it.[10]

So did the rest of the West. In this single speech, Roosevelt captured the attention of the West and, more significantly, vented the radical steam that Hoover's intransigence had built. Before, organizations
like the Nonpartisan League had been vehemently anti-Hoover but

more or less neutral about FDR. Suddenly, they became pro-Roosevelt. FDR ran up his biggest margins in the West, carrying every state in 1932. Throughout his administration he would consistently take 75 percent of the vote in the region.

The facile explanation, then, for the administration's immediate attention to the West is political debt, but there is more to the story. Roosevelt had more information to motivate action. For instance, the Federal Emergency Relief Administration sent the former Associated Press reporter Lorena Hickock on a tour of the region in 1933. Her handwritten dispatches made it straight back to the White House. Some examples:

> All I can say is that these people GOT to have clothing—RIGHT AWAY. It may be Indian Summer in Washington, but it's winter up here. They have had their first snow. . . .
> Into the relief office in Williston [North Dakota], county seat of Williams County, came today a middle-aged farmer—skin like leather, heavily calloused, grimy hands—incongruously attired in a worn light flannel suit of collegiate cut, flashy blue sweater, also worn, belted tan topcoat, a cap to match. These clothes, he explained, belonged to his eldest son.
> "They're all we got now," he said. "We take turns wearing 'em."

And this, also from North Dakota:

> In what was once a house I found two small boys, about two and four years old, running without a stitch on save some ragged overalls. . . . Their feet were purple with cold.
> You could see light under the door in that house. The kitchen floor was so patched up—with pieces of tin, a wash boiler cover, old automobile license plates—that you couldn't tell what it might have looked like originally. Plaster falling off the walls. Newspapers stuffed in the cracks around windows.
> The mother of those children—barelegged, although she had some ragged sneakers on her feet—is going to have another baby in January. IN THAT HOUSE. When she diffidently asked the [relief] investi-

gator who was with me for assurance that a doctor would be on hand to see her through her confinement, I could hardly bear it.

The investigator asked to see her bedding. She hesitated for a moment. Then led us upstairs. One iron bedstead. A filthy, ragged mattress, some dirty pillows—her bed linen, she said, all gave out more than a year ago—and a few old rags of blankets. Incidentally I heard yesterday of women having babies on beds with only coats thrown over them.

"Do you and your husband and the children all sleep in this bed?" the investigator asked. "We have to," she replied simply, "to keep warm."[11]

There was no lack of motive for the administration to fly into action, but the New Dealers did lack ideas. FDR came into power surrounded by a brain trust long on academics and short on specific and effective programs that it could ramp up immediately.

The Malta newspapers of the day occasionally included brief reports that the county extension agent Henry Lantz had traveled to Washington DC for yet another consultation with the federal government. He was probably meeting with Wilson, by then undersecretary of agriculture to Henry A. Wallace, and with a colleague of Wilson's from Montana State University, Elmer Starch, who had also joined the administration. In any event, Lantz finally received his money to carry out the Malta plan.

He began buying out dryland farmers and resettling the most skilled of them in experimental communities. But more than just dry farmers were involved in his dealings. Early in the program, the Malta paper carried a front-page editorial under the headline "Step in Boys, the Water Is Fine under the New Grazing Setup," advocating that not just farmers but also ranchers sell land to the government. This tied back to another key element of the Malta plan. Lantz proposed aggregating the land he bought back with remaining federal lands that had never been homesteaded, then leasing the combined acreage back to ranchers. The local paper saw this as a good deal for ranchers and advised them to sell their worst, most arid, most unproductive lands to the government but to keep their creek-bottom lands for raising hay and wheat. Then they could lease back their former lands for grazing. The deeds that remain today in Malta, the record of Lantz's work, show that ranchers did exactly as advised. Lantz's plan, the realities of arid lands, and the Depression that resulted reversed if not the nation's fundamental commitment to private property then the fact of private property. He was creating a commons.

⁓

The Malta newspaper published a flurry of front-page stories detailing Lantz's efforts, some of them under Lantz's byline, in particular, an article that was clear evidence of a showdown with the county's government.[12] Lantz used his space in March 1935 to report having acquired 583,000 acres of busted homesteads in Phillips County alone. Moreover, within the county there were 882,000 additional acres of federally owned land that had not been proved up. Also, the county possessed 308,000 acres it had taken for back taxes. The problem was, the county was balking on turning over its land to Lantz, so his page-one article threatened to scuttle the entire plan if the county didn't pony up. It did.

Lantz had big plans for the acquired land beyond the simple disposal of it. He intended to aggregate it—the federal land, the land he had bought, and the county's land—and use it just as the ranchers had in the Mizpah-Pumpkin Creeks experiment, that is, lease it to graziers at eight cents per cow-calf pair per month. A cow-calf pair needs at the very least forty acres in this region, and the graziers were then leasing county land for about two dollars an acre. As an accompanying editorial pointed out, owning the land cost a rancher more than two dollars an acre, as opposed to a cost of eight cents to lease forty acres.

Reports say Lantz was every bit as hands-on with the land acquisition as he was with local politics. He personally visited the farmer of each busted homestead, assessed his soil quality, classified his land, and offered a price. At the same time, he assessed the homesteaders' abilities. Those who passed muster were resettled on the irrigated land he had acquired, mostly around the town of Wagner, which was built from scratch with New Deal money. The paper carried almost weekly reports of the hammering and sawing on the planned community, work that employed dozens of men. The work on Wagner was but the beginning of the whole series of jobs that would attach to Lantz's plan, precisely why his work would capture the attention of the New Dealers in Washington. (Wagner, by the way, the planned community of stable farmers settled on small plots, is not much more than a highway sign today, mostly one big irrigated farm.)

The record of Lantz's work on the federal level supports the notion that he was not a man easily thwarted. Elmer Starch, the colleague of Wilson's who followed him to DC, recalled in 1953 that the name Lantz was well known, at least as high up as Rexford Tugwell. Lantz's behavior, in fact, landed Starch himself in hot water.

For some reason or other, I survived. I fought with Tugwell and lots of them. I wouldn't say for what reason, but there were clashes, which went all the way through the system—like Henry Lantz on the Milk River project in northern Montana. Henry was always full of action, he was getting things done, getting reservoirs built and irrigation land established and what not, but he was awfully impatient. He would give me hell if my office wasn't getting things done. When somebody from Washington came along, he'd do the same for them. Then it got reported in that Henry was disloyal, so I got a wire right away that said, "Fire Henry Lantz."

I wired back and said, "I'd like to know a little more about it." I had to see Henry anyway in a couple of days, and in a couple days more I'd be in Washington to discuss it more. Well we got along all through the years without having any of these men that were getting work done fired. Rex for some reason or other, would take my word for it, and didn't fire me.[13]

The "some reason" probably had to do with the viable ideas that Lantz, Starch, and Wilson had at a time when the administration was in a desperate search for solutions to the country's economic problems. "The question was: is there any way of relieving these people of their misery? . . . In the Great Plains there were any number of counties where 95 percent of the farmers were on relief," Starch recalled. "The most successful project . . . was what we know as the Milk River area, and the greatest man in reorganizing and reconstructing communities was a man named Henry Lantz. He had this idea of combining irrigated lands and surrounding grazing lands."[14]

Probably the best measure of the priority that the New Dealers gave Lantz's work was their sending in the biggest of guns to convince the locals. On August 9, 1934, the *Saco Independent*, the paper in Malta's neighboring town, carried the following headline regarding August 8: "President's Visit Monday Brings Out Thousands." FDR was in the Breaks officially to visit construction at the Fort Peck Dam, one of the major projects of the New Deal. But he had more than a dam on his mind. In his speech to eight thousand local farmers and ranchers, Roosevelt himself laid out the rationale for Henry Lantz's then budding program:

> It is a fact, however, you and I know there are many families in many states who are trying to make both ends meet without much success, because it has been shown over a period of years that the land that they are using for agriculture ought not, for the best economic purposes, be used for agriculture. Now if these families want to go on farming that land and going deeper into debt every year, that is their funeral; but on the other hand, your government believes in giving them a chance to go to better places and farm this land and that is why our national planning is seeking to provide much smaller farms, but farms where you won't be faced with starvation.

Mark this. In all previous federal administrations the a priori rule was to settle homesteaders on every bit of public, unforested land. At this level, there had never been a policy that farming might somehow be uneconomic anywhere, but the Depression was nothing if not an illustration of agriculture's diseconomies, both in the market sense and in the deeper sense of the economy of nature.

Had Lantz's work remained just his—a visionary's experiment on a forgotten corner of the plains—it still would have been important enough to remember today. All told, Lantz's project eventually covered seven million acres in three counties. He resettled nine hundred families. Fast-forward for a moment to the project that is the concern of this book: acquiring and restoring the prairie lands around the Missouri Breaks. Its scope of 3.5 million acres is breathtaking, unprecedented in modern conservation, yet this vast area equals exactly half of Lantz's project. The modern project would affect about fifty ranching families, not nine hundred. Lantz's project bought a total of about a million acres of private land; the prairie project plans to buy eight hundred thousand acres. Indeed, the scope of the prairie project does have precedent, in fact, in this very spot. This is not coincidence but rather is wound into the arid facts of the place. Lantz began the work that this generation must finish.

But Lantz's work was only a beginning during the New Deal as well. All that communication with DC was for a reason. The New Deal seized on the project and formalized it first as the Land Utilization Program, borrowing the term Wilson had used in his outline of FDR's campaign speech. Then it morphed into the Resettlement Administration, which was Tugwell's pet project and the one that drew most of his energies after 1935. It began that year with twelve employees but had sixteen thousand only two years later. Nationwide, the program bought back 11.3 million acres' worth of busted homesteads for $47.5 million, almost all of them in the West.[15] These lands were aggregated with unsettled lands, as they had been in Phillips County, and leased to graziers, but first a mechanism had to be in place for doing so. The Mizpah-Pumpkin Creeks experiment had to scale up throughout the West.

⋘

Before the New Deal, one of the stalwarts in the defeat of legislation to allow grazing on public lands had been a conservative Republican congressman from Colorado, Edward Taylor, who thought public lands grazing a form of socialism, and indeed it was a contradiction of the nation's long-standing commitment to privatizing public property.

The urgencies of the Dust Bowl coupled with growth in the stock of public lands, not their reduction, which had motivated passage of the Homestead Act, brought a new round of support for a grazing bill. It was, in fact, a keystone of the New Deal, part of the Progressives' policy of conservation. The administration quickly scored something of a coup in helping to push this plan through Congress by enlisting the support of Taylor, who had done a complete about-face after a tour of the ravaged grazing lands of the Dust Bowl West. Taylor testified in Congress in support of his bill: "On the western slope of Colorado and in nearby states I saw waste, competition, overuse, and abuse of valuable range lands and watersheds eating into the very heart of the western economy. Farms and ranches everywhere in the range country were suffering. The basic economy of entire communities was threatened. There was terrific strife and bloodshed between the cattle and sheep men over the use of the range."[16]

The law that bears his name, the Taylor Grazing Act, a pivotal point of American public lands policy, passed Congress in April 1934, the same month that the dust clouds rolled into Washington DC. It was viewed as a conservation measure, in fact, the very essence of Progressive policy in the West. It established what was supposed to have been a grazing commons managed by ranchers as a sort of cooperative landscape. Ranchers formed large, often county-sized grazing districts and would jointly run cattle on them on the basis of local conditions and local decisions about key factors, such as stocking rates.

This is not simply an isolated story of the New Deal or a forgotten corner of Montana. It is *the* story of the American West. Lantz clones spread out across the plains and acquired 11.3 million acres of busted homesteads. This acreage was aggregated with lands that had never been homesteaded to amass 307 million acres of public lands leased to graziers in eleven western states, 41 percent of the total land base in those states. This is larger than the combined areas of Maine, New Hampshire, Vermont, Massachusetts, Connecticut, New York, New Jersey, Pennsylvania, Maryland, Virginia, West Virginia, Kentucky, Ohio, Indiana, and Michigan.

The New Dealers, however, were not content simply to buy the land. The acquisition provided a sort of land base for a massive commitment to public works. That is, the administration could put people to work under programs such as the Works Progress Administration and the Civilian Conservation Corps to "improve" those lands.

⁀

In the early spring of 2004, a heavy March snow left the prairie covered in deep, mushy drifts and the few roads converted to a sticky mire of clay the locals call "gumbo." Travel was iffy, even in my Jeep, which was caked in a solid exoskeleton of gumbo, but I had driven eight hours east out of my home in Missoula and was not about to let some mud thwart my mission to find Gene Barnard at his isolated ranch fifty miles south of Malta. Everyone I had talked to told me I ought to talk to Gene about the Breaks. He had an avocation for history, knew the local tales, and, at eighty-four, was old enough to remember well more than half of the settled history of the place.

Gene, a genial old man, a rancher in overalls and flannel shirts, offered me a seat in the kitchen of his modest frame house. The owner of a ranch running to maybe fifty thousand acres, Gene is a millionaire on paper, but nothing in the surroundings would suggest this. He was glad to see a visitor because he had been snowed in for the couple of weeks previous. No mail. An ancient TV set blared game shows in the next room. The kitchen itself was piled one end to the other with dishes, food boxes and cans, syringes for doctoring calves, muddy boots, and winter coats.

Barnard ran me through an account of the place's history since settlement, beginning with some details such as precise locations of Granville Stuart's first hay meadows and the cottonwoods that served as gibbets for his stranglers. It was his personal recollection of the Great Depression, though, that served as my first tip that something big had happened here during the 1930s, a period Barnard remembers well, mostly as a lonely time. He was often left alone on his father's ranch for long periods while the rest of the family was away building ponds. The feds, Lantz's colleagues, hired many of the local ranchers to build stock ponds on the lands they had acquired from those very ranchers in many cases.

This fetish for ponds tracks all the way to FDR himself, who often advised western politicians to run on the slogan "A pond for every farm." In one of his famous fireside chats, that of September 6, 1936, he said the relief work on ponds on the plains was a necessity "to supply water for stock and to lift the level of the underground water to protect wells from going dry." If that was the goal, the ranchers of the Breaks got more than their measure. Today in this arid landscape, an artificial pond exists on almost every square mile of the five thousand square miles of Phillips County. This was the New Deal's solution to aridity, making up for short rains by building storage, something like dealing with poverty by giving wall safes to the poor.

This is a matter of no small environmental consequence. Arid landscapes such as the short-grass prairie live and breathe only because they are veined with small streams that hold water. Those streams and only those streams raise streamside vegetation like willows and wild rose, which provide key habitat for most of the wildlife. Birds nest there. Deer feed and hide their fawns. But more important, the riparian vegetation forms a protective cover over the stream, sheltering it from sun and dry winds. Stream water, trapped and left in an open pond, simply evaporates. Those ponds, which are really impoundments of the streams, have robbed virtually every stream on the Missouri Breaks of its water. Riparian vegetation, already badly bruised by cattle, is virtually nonexistent.

FDR's commitment to ponds, however, was about much more than water. The Malta paper, for instance, reported that twelve hundred men in Phillips County were at work building ponds. Today, fewer than twelve hundred employable males live in the county. And in a sense, the pond construction was necessary. Barnard is unequivocal: The Great Depression was the roughest period of his eighty-four years in the Breaks, and he says his family made it through only because of those wages for building ponds. The ponds were not the end for the New Deal; the wages were. In its first year, the program for grazing land employed twelve thousand men regionwide. By 1939, the Civilian Conservation Corps alone had built 358 spring developments, 143 wells with storage facilities, 780 earth reservoirs, 1,950 miles of range fences, and 225 corrals and had poisoned prairie dogs and ground squirrels on 7.3 million acres.[17]

David Rivenes was a New Deal worker based in Miles City, which is southeast of the Breaks. In an oral history interview, he recalled that pond building was a major activity there as well. He says the program was forced to work with a design for those ponds handed down from Washington DC, a design the locals suspected wouldn't work but were not allowed to change. He said at least a third of the dams that held the ponds washed out in a year or two, but that was okay with his bosses. Administrators of the program were held accountable not for the quality of the dams but for the number of men put to work immediately.

The work was not limited to dams, as we've seen; federal money also built facilities the ranchers and homesteaders couldn't afford to build when they owned the land, for example, corrals, fences, and dipping vats. That is, the New Deal provided not only the land but also the infrastructure of the grazing industry. Recall that the feds spent $47.5 million to buy the land. They spent more than twice that, $103 million, on make-work infrastructure projects, "improvements."

None of this was seen as a handout to the industry. On the contrary, it was a federal government serving its role to build sustainable communities in the West. Tugwell was among the clearest on this, repeatedly stating that the work was nothing if not scientific, that the government would launch a program, then closely monitor results to see what worked and then adjust until the program efficiently served the public good. All of this was, as M. L. Wilson's earlier experimental communities had been, social engineering, but on the scale of half a continent. The programs had the twin goals of conservation and social justice. Yet the land had a different idea; the work did nothing to stop the long-term trend of depopulation.

In his oral history interview, David Rivenes recounted this:

> One of the things we did was decide to build a rec center in Prairie County [just southeast of Phillips County]. It was all done with WPA labor. We built tennis courts, dammed a lake for boating and swimming, horseshoe pitching courts, a softball diamond, an archery range and a very, very nice big hall that had not only a big dance floor but a stage, and it had a kitchen in the basement. It also had shower baths. Everything. It was very, very nice, but the catch to all this was the government had bought up all the submarginal land and was resettling the people off the land on irrigation projects that were being constructed, many with WPA labor. People got jobs building that great big recreation center. Then when the job was done everybody moved, and there wasn't anybody to use the recreation center. Everybody had been bought off. It was the dog gonedest thing. It was crazy that it should work out this way, but that's the way it was. There it sat with practically no one for miles around.[18]

Eight

THE UNWILD WEST

By late October [1934], the government had spent nearly $525 million in a single year to save the cattlemen from ruin and starvation. For this salvation, many cattlemen never forgave the government. . . . History is one thing, legends are another. Nothing is so striking in the records of the plains cattle industry as the divergence between the history and the legend. Cattlemen have always seen themselves as fiercely independent, neither seeking nor receiving help from anyone, and certainly not getting help from the government. They represent themselves, without guile and without deceit, as the last-surviving defenders of ancient American liberties. Oddly, most Americans do not even take offense at these airs. Yet the slightest glance at the record reveals countless efforts by the cattlemen to get governmental assistance of one sort or another. They continually sought help and they often got it. This is true, and it is neither bad nor good, just true.

— *Historian John T. Schlebecker, 1963*

There were mouthy individuals who seized every opportunity to run down the entire program . . . condemning it as useless, crooked, revolutionary, or dictatorial; but . . . when the first AAA [the New Deal's Agricultural Adjustment Act] payments were made available, shortly before Christmas, these same wordy critics made a beeline to the courthouse. They jostled and fell over each other in their mad scramble to be the first in line to receive allotment money.

— *Lawrence Svobida, a Kansas farmer recalling the New Deal*

When watching a judo match, we can easily believe not much is happening. The ancient and cerebral martial art is an exercise in incrementalism. A combatant gains gradual advantage through an opponent's mistakes, especially by harnessing the energy of an opponent's initiatives and using that energy against him. The object is to work an opponent slowly toward defeat, as a ratchet works a bolt, taking up any slack an opponent's mistake allows but never giving back that slack when the opponent recovers. Finally a dramatic and definitive throw comes, an unmistakable victory, but it has been set up in a series of persistent, unseen moves.

Special-interest politics gives a judolike advantage to the special interests. Those charged with defending the general interest must pay attention to a wide array of forces and demands, but special interests can be single-minded. They can capitalize on the mistakes of their distracted opponents to gain advantage slowly, taking up a bit of slack each time, unnoticed by the casual observer.

This is what happened to the good intentions of the Taylor Grazing Act. What started as a program to promote conservation and community has become in our time the largest threat to the environment of the American West. A modern conservationist ignorant of history is incredulous at hearing that the act was a brainchild of the New Deal's sincere conservationists. How can that be, when it is the act that virtually privatized most of the grassland West's public lands? The cattlemen used the mistakes of their opponents to their advantage, unobserved over a generation, to effect a 180-degree turn in the act's intent. The mistakes of the New Dealers were not so much the result of their motives as the result of their failures in execution, rooted equally in a single and colossal mistake by Roosevelt himself, in the pettiness of personal politics, and in the global upheaval of World War II.

Franklin Roosevelt, arguably the most skilled politician ever to occupy the White House, rarely made mistakes. He was a genius at manipulating and orchestrating his opponents as well as the diverse and intense body of advisers who surrounded him. A favorite tactic of his was one unthinkable in our time. He let cabinet members wage very public wars with one another in the press over substantive issues. He would often appear to agree with each side and in the end would use the public reaction the controversy engendered to decide an issue. This very messy and public debate evolved in a time of immense and overwhelming crisis, the very sorts of situations that have caused modern administrations such as that of George W. Bush to invoke unprecedented levels of secrecy. FDR's solution to the crisis of democracy was more democracy.

In this sort of free-for-all, he launched and landed the most ambitious legislative agenda in the history of his office, at least during that crucial first term. Yet in doing so, he made enemies. For instance, one of the more revolutionary programs came through his Department of the Interior, especially at the behest of Interior secretary Harold Ickes. Ickes is a standout in this cabinet of standouts, a man who, I will argue in the next chapter, made conservation as we know it possible. He is also an interesting personal link to the Progressive movement, which, recall, began in the Republican Party under Theodore Roosevelt. Ickes was then a Chicago city official, thoroughly urban, and an unlikely candidate to become the nation's chief advocate for conservation. He was also an adamant supporter of Theodore Roosevelt and, like many, bolted from the Republican Party when TR split off the Progressive wing to run as an independent Bull Moose candidate.

During the Progressive genesis, Ickes—largely through his first wife, a wealthy Chicago socialite—developed an interest in the plight of American Indians. When he assumed office at the Department of the Interior, he very quickly translated that interest into the most enlightened policy toward American Indians the country had ever seen. He appointed a longtime ally and a champion of Indian rights, Harold Collier, to run Indian affairs in 1933.

Collier quickly promulgated a special New Deal for Indians, including legislation to halt the widespread sale of Indian lands. Those sales were at the time predatory in that the Indians were so impoverished by the Depression that they had no other recourse but to sell their land to whites. Social workers dispatched by the FDR administration to assess the situation on reservations found them, predictably enough, even worse off than their white neighbors. The government documented appalling poverty, including widespread malnutrition and epidemics of whooping cough, tuberculosis, and trachoma.

Collier's and Ickes's efforts faced increasing opposition through the years, especially from key western senators and, among them, especially from Burton K. Wheeler, a liberal Democrat from Montana. Wheeler had been among FDR's staunchest supporters in 1932; Roosevelt personally credited him with delivering landslide support in Montana. Yet the racism of the West, which is only slightly diminished today, helped split people like Wheeler from the New Deal. The issue, in fact, grew increasingly contentious and ugly, with Collier eventually facing charges of un-Americanism and Communism for his efforts on reservations. Both Ickes's and Collier's membership in the American Civil Liberties Union became an issue. By 1937, the West's split from the New Deal was so complete that Wheeler began working for the repeal of the Indian Reorganization Act, the primary vehicle for Collier's reforms.

The abdication of the West's politicians, however, was not the lone wedge splitting off FDR's western power base. Two more major rifts occurred, one of which remains to this day one of the largest impediments to a rational and streamlined approach to public lands conservation in the United States and ties directly to a decision made in Theodore Roosevelt's administration. Gifford Pinchot's belief that forestry was something like farming—a husbanding of trees to allow their "wise use," by which he meant logging—resulted in his organizational strategy to have TR include Pinchot's department of forestry not in a public lands office of the Department of the Interior but in the Department of Agriculture. We have already seen how this allowed Pinchot to play off ranchers against other forces, such as loggers and miners, to create forest reserves, which, as you recall, were established primarily to protect high-elevation watersheds so that they might feed irrigation.

Part of Pinchot's political manipulation established a more informal system that also survives. The forest reserves, now national forests, actually became the private political preserves of western state senators. Today in the West but also elsewhere to a degree, an all-but-official rule forbids anything happening in any given state's national forests unless the delegation of that state allows it. As late as the 1980s, when I was a political reporter for a western newspaper, I watched this rule work, demonstrating that an individual senator could scuttle years of painstaking negotiations on issues such as wilderness designation with the flick of a wrist.

In the early twentieth century this sort of power meant patronage, the currency of politics, the measure of political capital. Early in the New Deal, Ickes began to understand fully the real implications of this system. Part of the administration of public lands, the unsettled lands, was his business in the Department of the Interior, whereas the administration of forested public lands fell to Henry Wallace and the Department of Agriculture. It didn't help that the two were often at odds. So Ickes proposed the creation of a department of conservation, which would administer all public lands, the simple, straightforward, and rational step that conservationists today would still like to accomplish but have given up striving for. The vested interests know well this divide-and-conquer strategy that the separate arrangement allows, so they resist this vital reform. FDR biographer Frank Freidel has analyzed the problem: "As various congressmen expressed dismay over the likelihood of losing patronage or some cherished relationship with a government agency they helped oversee, the overriding issue became apparent. They saw reorganization as weakening their own power and prerogatives in relation to those of the president."[1]

The resistance then was even more pronounced than it is today and was spearheaded by no less than Pinchot himself, by that time an angry and ego-poisoned old man. Pinchot arose from his retirement like a specter from the grave and used his anger and his bureaucratic abilities to rally opposition to any tampering with his beloved U.S. Forest Service, his monument. Rallying the opposition was easy; Pinchot knew full well how dependent western lawmakers were on the patronage created on Forest Service lands, by then aswarm with thousands on thousands of New Deal workers, such as those of the Civilian Conservation Corps. That is, what was then emerging as the opposition to the New Deal was being fueled with New Deal money, the energy of a New Deal initiative. The public lands were the land base of patronage. In the end, FDR needed the votes of two western senators on a key piece of legislation so, in trade for those votes, promised not to create Ickes's department of conservation, which the western senators despised. One wedge driven.

The bigger split, however, was spurred by a watershed situation during the prewar years of the administration: Roosevelt's scheme to deal with a reactionary U.S. Supreme Court that was systematically scuttling his sweeping legislative agenda as unconstitutional. It was, unlike Pinchot's pettiness, a real issue. FDR responded to the country's crisis by wielding all of his power and then some. He was becoming, in the view of his more thoughtful opponents, a benign dictator. The more bitter among the opposition openly dropped the adjective *benign*. The Supreme Court was checking and balancing.

In 1937, Roosevelt proposed a unique idea to deal with this. He would use a loophole to appoint as many extra and friendly Supreme Court justices as he needed to swing the majority in his direction, a scheme that came to be called "court packing." The scheme failed and enraged the opposition in the process. Roosevelt's own vice president, John Nance Garner, openly opposed it. Montana's Burton K. Wheeler led the opposition.

In the meantime, while all this turmoil churned domestic issues, the master of politics was becoming increasingly distracted, increasingly above the fray. The opposition didn't know it in the late 1930s, but FDR's attention was riveted on global events. Perhaps the charge of dictator applies best to what he was doing on this front. Without the consent of Congress, without direction, he was secretly gearing up to go to war with Europe's fascists. He alone correctly read the dire nature of the threat and unilaterally, in a clear overreaching of his constitutional powers, made the nation ready for it. When we entered World War II officially in 1941, his single-minded action undoubtedly made it winnable by the Allies.

The Taylor Grazing Act, sweeping as it was, seems almost trivial in this context, and that is exactly the point. It was keystone legislation when it was passed in the halcyon days of the New Deal, in 1934. But it had to be implemented, had to be worked out in a very different national environment. The New Deal had lost its support, not among westerners, but among western lawmakers, and the administration was facing a world war.

⤞

The Palace Theater still stands in Malta, now a retail shop with the same deserted and forlorn look of those around it. Yet in 1934, according to the report of the *Phillips County News*, it was anything but deserted during a day-long meeting on December 4: "Interest in the proposal is indicated by the fact that the theater was jammed to the doors both morning and afternoon, and many were unable to get in at all."[2]

It was mostly jammed with ranchers, with one standout exception: F. R. Carpenter, whom Ickes had named to head the new U.S. Grazing Service. Something momentous was transpiring. The quiet experiment at Mizpah and Pumpkin creeks, which Lantz had visited only seven years before, had cut the pattern for Lantz's experiment in Phillips County, and now the experiment had been encoded in national law passed that spring, the Taylor Grazing Act. Carpenter was there to explain the act to the gathered ranchers but also to witness the creation of Grazing District Number One, the first.

Apparently, the assemblage did not need a lot of convincing to endorse this big government program. The vote at the Palace Theater was 474 to 9 in favor. This was in the early days of Taylor, when it was still a program for conservation, still an idealist experiment that regarded the federal land as federal land. All that began to change almost immediately. In Phillips County and in two adjacent counties, the experiment reestablished the open range. That is, the millions of acres of public lands were not fenced or divided up among the ranchers. Each had the right to graze a certain number of cattle, sheep, or horses on the entire commons. This provision is pivotal.

The evolution of the Taylor Grazing Act proceeded generally as channeled by the forces outlined above, but specifically by the machinations of Senator Patrick McCarran, of Nevada, a state that is about two-thirds federal land, so was then and is now a flash point for clashes surrounding grazing issues. The historian Louise Peffer wrote: "The Taylor Grazing Act was not perfect. Nevertheless, its basic imperfections were not so great as to account for its failure. The fact that it had been rendered virtually useless except in protecting the interest of licensed graziers is attributable to several causes, chiefly the feud among the conservationists, the war and Senator Patrick McCarran."[3]

McCarran, a demi-demagogue, forced the administration to compromise, not only on the act itself, but also on a series of amendments to the act that accrued during the immediate decade after it was passed. The first of those was a preference clause, giving ranchers living adjacent to federal lands a sort of squatter's right to lease those lands. Ickes opposed that clause, but his boss forced him to compromise. More critical was a provision adopted in 1939 that empowered locally elected boards, the ranchers themselves, to administer completely their own districts. Late in life, Carpenter said, "Ickes approved [the local boards] with tongue in cheek, believing they would keep the heat off him and that he could abolish them as soon as the reorganization was complete."[4]

Even without tongue in cheek, Ickes meant for the boards to serve as specified: as advisory. The cattlemen had another idea, and in 1940, acting as a national organization, they were successful in winning a centralized version of the local boards, a national advisory board, also made up of graziers and others from the industry. By this time, the administration was distracted by the war and was making the incremental mistakes that grant advantage in a judo match. The cattlemen quietly went about playing their advantage.

The crucial step in exercising the power was to give the local advisory boards control over the income from the leasing fees and the ability to set those fees. In practice, control over the budget gave the ranchers control over the federal staff that was to enforce the rules and prevent overgrazing. "In effect, the regulators were being supervised by those who were to be regulated," wrote the historian Phillip O. Foss.[5]

The move effectively created a positive feedback loop. The ranchers, who were by now setting their own fees, wanted to keep fees low, and, obviously, by keeping fees low, they also ensured insufficient money to hire more staff, that is, regulators. There would be no federal presence to protect against abuses such as overgrazing. Just as important, the autonomy the grazing boards won through this series of compromises created a closed loop; the federal lands leased produced no revenue stream to the federal treasury. By capturing all the revenue, the local boards had, in effect, privatized the federal lands or at least appropriated them for the local grazing districts. The national stock growers organizations, in fact, formalized this principle with a policy statement in 1946: "Paying a fee for revenue [to the federal treasury] . . . is contrary to the fundamentals on which this country was built."[6] By then, the stock growers were literally writing the laws that governed them, and this proviso became part of those laws.

This switch came during a pivotal year. Carpenter's Grazing Service was combined with the old Public Lands Office in 1946 to form the Bureau of Land Management, the agency that still, at least nominally, superintends grazing on federal lands, controlling an area larger than France, twice the size of Japan.

There remained but one step in completely gutting the Taylor Grazing Act, and that came two decades into the process of reforming the act. The bureaucracy adopted a measure that split, fenced, and attached allotments to individual ranches; that is, the land was no longer a commons. The measure reversed the act's pivotal provision. Today, it is not at all uncommon to hear a rancher in the Breaks say he ranches forty-five thousand acres, but he needs to be pressed for the qualifying clause: "five thousand deeded and forty thousand leased," a typical ratio. In other words, he owns maybe 15 percent of his land base. The American public owns the rest, but you wouldn't know it to look at it.

Writing in 1960, Foss summarized this evolution of grazing law: "It would appear that, primarily through the administrative process, a small interest group has been able to establish a kind of private government with reference to the federal grazing districts. It would appear that they formulate the broad policy, make the rules, and superintend the execution of these rules and policies."[7] On the surface, this appears very much like privatization, but we know privatization was the goal of the Homestead Act of 1862, and it, in fact, failed dramatically here. The government spent more than a century trying to give this land away but ended up buying much of it back. This is far more than a failure of policy or administration; it is a failure of the fundamental principle of private property, an idea defeated by arid landscapes. Private property is about borders, about drawing lines, but grassland animals and grassland people are nomadic, and for a reason. Local droughts, storms, bad years, and dust bowls require that they be able to move to better places. Borders work against this motion, and freedom of motion enables life in the arid West to survive.

The plains are only the biggest and most glaring example of the failure of the idea of private property, not just in the West, but in much of the Midwest as well. The truth is, the subsidy represented by the below-market grazing fees and the gift of land is but a very small part of the program of subsidies to American agriculture. The nation now spends about twenty billion dollars a year in direct crop subsidies, almost all of this money allocated to the landscape between the Mississippi River and the Rocky Mountains. Without federal subsidy, Montana's net agricultural income—the largest sector of the state's economy—would be zero. Almost all of the programs that evolved into this massive system of subsidies began during the New Deal. This system is not what the Progressives intended. They had in mind helping starving children, the Tom Joads, but those subsidy checks today mostly go to wealthy corporate megafarms. The very heart of subsidy land is the red-state West and Midwest, populated by a bunch of flag-waving, bellowing conservatives who proclaim their rugged independence on clutters of stickers plastered onto the bumpers of behemoth pickup trucks bought with crop support payments for wheat.

There's an odd sort of bottom line to all of this that is not anomaly but rather a direct result of this very system. The *Washington Post* reported the following in 2005: "The latest report from the Tax Foundation show[s] how much each state gets back in contracts, benefits and subsidies for every dollar of taxes paid. And it shows that, with a few exceptions, the anti-government red states are the net winners in the flow of funds while the pro-government blue states are almost all losers."[8] The American West is a welfare state. The joke in Phillips County is that a rancher can double his income by erecting a second mailbox.

Something more fundamentally American than private property has emerged. That is, we can survive here as westerners only by substituting what has become the fundamental principle of America. We privatize profits, and we socialize risks. We are parasites.

A rule of biology is: If a resource accrues in excess, a species will evolve the skills to exploit it. The New Dealers, with the best of motives, created just such a resource, a big, centralized, and powerful system for dispensing federal money. Then came the distractions of politics and war, and that big machine was left idling at the curb. It was a simple matter to hijack it and drive it away. A new species, welfare ranching, evolved. It has the protective coloration of the myth of private property to disguise its parasitic nature.

❦

Ranching towns of the plains are generally not much more than a strip along the highway. Amenities include at least a café, a bar (named either Stockman's or Sportsman's), a convenience store that sells diesel fuel and bad coffee, and maybe a forlorn little church. This is the minimum, and most ranching towns don't bother with much more.

Mornings find a string of muddy, diesel-powered, four-wheel-drive pickup trucks, most with compact black-and-white border collies, working cattle dogs, waiting patiently in the back of the truck, perched on a tool box or a pile of shovels, fence supplies, and ropes. There's one large table inside the café, and it is ringed with a jovial bunch of big men in Carhartt working clothes and, at least in winter, billed and ear-floppered Elmer Fudd hats. As each enters, he walks across the café to the coffee pot in the corner, fills his own mug, and joins the circle, usually greeted by an inside joke shot in his direction. The talk is of weather or last Friday's high school football game (eight-man here; the high schools are too small to field eleven).

A stranger who gets out of the newer car in the parking lot, a car with city plates (Montana car registrations are coded by county), is eyed, even greeted, by all but knows to take a seat separately at a small corner table to suffer the coffee, and he is soon forgotten by the assembled. He eavesdrops, of course. Hard not to; the ranchers josh each other in booming country voices.

I was struck that morning by how much ranch talk runs to killing or eradicating offensive bits of nature. This one morning that I describe here occurred at a wide-spot-in-the-road town in Montana's Musselshell River Valley, and the talk was mostly about deer. The river provides a sinuous strip of riparian habitat through the valley, and at dawn and dusk of any day, the landscape is alive with deer, mostly white-tail, but mule deer as well. Antelope dot the uplands. The ranchers are interested in seeing these animals driven off or eradicated, and they generally welcome as many hunters as arrive. This is not at all malicious. In the next town up, for instance, an albino deer appeared one year, and the locals were successful in lobbying the state for a special regulation that forbade the killing of white deer. The enmity toward deer is less malicious than it is a matter of survival. Deer, antelope, and elk can gobble up prodigious amounts of grass and hay meant for cattle. They nibble at the thin edge of profit margin.

The considerable irony in this, of course, is that those wild ungulates are perfectly successful in converting grass to protein. Many Montana residents, including me, depend on rancher hospitality allowing us access to hunt a freezer full of protein every fall, a year's meat for the price of a few rifle shells and a tank of gas, an economic bargain both in the monetary sense and in the deeper and more important sense of efficient conversion of energy. It's sustainable.

The ranchers expend no small amount of effort in driving off and otherwise eradicating big hunks of wild protein so that they might raise domestic protein, really feeder calves. These calves are rounded up each fall and sent off to feedlots in corn belt states, where they stand shoulder to shoulder for a year, belly deep in their own manure and fattening on a stream of corn and antibiotics, providing the cholesterol-laden slabs of marbled beef that, for all consumers know, begins and ends as a shrink-wrapped package at the Safeway. I'll take the venison.

None of this, of course, is the ranchers' fault. As we have seen, America learned a sobering lesson about market hunting during the nineteenth century. Virtually all of conservation in most of the twentieth was geared toward recovery of populations of deer, elk, antelope, and game birds such as ducks and geese, which had been hunted to the edge of extinction by devices such as punt guns, giant shotguns that felled whole flocks in a single blast. Market hunting is now a cultural taboo.

The result of this taboo is not just an abundance of deer but a dangerous excess of them, especially in riparian areas of the West but even more so in the more humid states of the Northeast. Pennsylvania and New Jersey, for instance, are awash in unhunted deer. In Michigan, the state where I was raised, deer have become so overpopulated that they are stunted. The animals have grown noticeably smaller in one human generation.

Meanwhile, ranchers have no legal means to profit from deer and elk, to market their protein, other than from hosting the odd bit of fee hunting and boarding a few hunters. Further, sports hunters tend to be highly selective toward large males, so the population has become greatly skewed to does and fawns. All of this leaves the ranchers with a glut of wildlife that has to be dealt with one way or another.

You recall the language of Granville Stuart, the pioneer cattleman of Montana who moved big herds into the areas south of the Breaks in the 1880s. He and all the other cattlemen were then grazing on federal land to which they had no legal right. Yet his sense of entitlement to that land—and to even more than that—rings in the language of his memoir. Stuart repeatedly laments the government's failure to deal with "its" Indians, who did in fact have a claim to some of the land. His writings and also the stockman's association he helped form made repeated requests for federal troops to stave off depredations at the same time the ranchers were making a good bit of income supplying those federal troops with horses and beef.

Stuart was not an aberration but an archetype. The tone of entitlement continues. While it began as a war on the native human life of the plains, it quickly extended to a war on all native life, a battle that continues. Ranchers believe it is the government's responsibility to deal with "its" nature, especially its wildlife. This expectation of government control was formalized as early as 1911, when stockmen officially began lobbying the U.S. Biological Survey, the organization then charged with studying and protecting wildlife, to eradicate prairie dogs. And such pleas were not limited to the plains' ubiquitous rodents. Nor were they without effect. Between 1915 and 1918, just three years, the biological survey, at government expense, exterminated 60,473 coyotes, 8,094 bobcats, and 1,829 wolves.[9]

The federal government first formed an agency called Animal Damage Control in 1886 as a part of the Department of Agriculture, but it served then mostly to disseminate information, that is, to educate farmers on ways to eradicate pests. The ranchers' lobbying in the 1910s radically changed that mission. Congress made a major appropriation, and the agency took on the job of doing the actual killing, the result being the exterminations itemized above.

In 1921, the government opened a laboratory at Denver charged with inventing new methods of slaughter, a function it still performs. By 1930, the work had become controversial, coming under its first of many formal attacks from scientific groups, then the Society of Mammalogists. This did not stop President Hoover from signing a law in 1931 giving the agency the statutory authority under which it still operates. The agency has been moved from the Department of Agriculture to the Interior and back again, has come under repeated frontal assaults in a long series of government reports and studies, one headed by no less than Starker Leopold, Berkeley professor of zoology and oldest son of conservationist Aldo Leopold, and yet it remains. The noticeable response to criticism has been a rebranding in 1997, from Damage Control to Wildlife Services, yet the euphemism is not much of a fig leaf. The killing continues to the tune of at least ten million dollars a year. That's the federal contribution. And that appropriation has been repeatedly bolstered by appropriations from state and local governments.

Throughout its history, the eradication has concentrated heavily on top-end predators, many of which prey most heavily on the deer and antelope that plague ranchers or on the prairie dogs and other rodents they poison. No matter that biologists now understand that, because of their position atop the food chain, top-end predators are the most threatened of species and the most difficult to preserve. Nothing has changed.

In 1999 the agency performed its service for wildlife by killing 589 badgers, 342 bears, 2,419 bobcats, 85,262 coyotes, 5,531 foxes, and

359 mountain lions. Besides the wanton carnage these numbers represent, we can view this picture another way. The numbers seem huge, but ironically they represent not a great deal of bang for the buck. Overall, the cost of killing predators exceeds livestock losses from predators by three to one. One case, cited by the authors Brooks Fahy and Cheri Briggs, is particularly illustrative.[10] The television news celebrity Sam Donaldson happens to be among the growing list of wealthy hobby ranchers in the West. His spread is in New Mexico, where he raises sheep. At Donaldson's request, federal officials visited his ranch a total of 412 times in the five-year period beginning in 1991. The agency logged a total of 178 staff days in this service. In the meantime, Donaldson, the millionaire rancher, reported sheep losses totaling thirty-one hundred dollars, probably less than he made for a single standup at the White House.

Part of the reason this whole business is so inefficient relates to the methods perfected at places like the Denver lab. The standout among them is aerial slaughter, by which the agency means air strikes on wildlife. Using mostly helicopters but also some fixed-wing aircraft, agents fly over the lands of a complaining rancher, blasting away with shotguns and rifles at any offending predator. Those 1999 numbers included 30,875 coyotes killed in this fashion, as well as 390 bobcats, 231 foxes, and 3 badgers. A fox is not much bigger than a house cat, nor is a badger. Both prey primarily on prairie dogs, which are also eradicated at the expense of taxpayers.

Meanwhile, taxpayers pay between two hundred and eight hundred dollars for each coyote death, depending on conditions. In native American lore, coyotes often serve the all-important role of trickster, an apt title in this case. Biologists now know that coyotes have an almost teleological ability to adjust their birth rates by producing larger litters when populations are low, as when their numbers have been thinned by aircraft.

The agency has less glamorous means at its disposal. It also kills with leghold traps; a method called "denning," which wipes out pups before they emerge from dens; hunting dogs; and an array of poisons, especially one particularly lethal to canines called "compound 1080." It is odorless when laced in meat baits left around the range. This and sodium cyanide make for a certain amount of collateral damage. A study in 1998 confirmed poisons meant for coyotes that year had killed 1,277 foxes (a nontarget animal then), 267 domestic dogs, 253 raccoons, and a gray wolf, that is, a member of an endangered species.[11]

There was once in the Breaks and the rest of the plains a slight little fox called the swift fox. Early explorers report it as being bold, willing to venture, albeit warily, into camp for handouts. The swift fox somehow became a casualty of all this wildlife damage control, through trapping but also as a result of invasion by alien predators such as the red fox, which has moved in to fill niches now vacant of the coyote and the wolf. In 1967, someone thought to tape-record an interview with a long-time cowboy in the Breaks, Billie Spencer. He recalled the following:

> We'd camp up there the other side of Beaver [Creek], and there was this animal. They called him a swift's—looked like a little fox—and he'd come around your camp at night and you'd sit right quiet and have a little fire going and see these two bright eyes shining. You'd throw out a little piece of bacon or a little piece of bread and sit still, and it'd dart in and snatch it up, and away it'd go. You don't see them anymore. They're gone. They lived in old badger holes, and they could really run for about a hundred feet. The last one I saw was in '28.[12]

It is possible that Spencer is wrong. The swift fox and all those other animals so effectively controlled with guns, grazing, poison, and leghold traps may not be gone. It may be possible to refill the vacuum.

Nine

CONSERVATION'S CONTRADICTION

Pinchot's work for conservation between 1897 and 1909 is his monument. Even before his dismissal, power and arrogance had warped his
sense of proportion. After the rupture of his relations with Taft and
his loss of official status, his policy was based on thwarted ambition,
bitterness and determination for revenge, which made most of his subsequent "conservation" activities a tragic travesty of his first achievements. . . . There was something frenzied and pathetic in Pinchot's
anger. Conservation under his leadership had become a cult.

—*Historian Louise Peffer*

The drive south from Malta to the Breaks today offers the impression
that one is headed toward the edge of the world. It covers about sixty
miles of beaten-up gravel road on which one is likely to encounter
maybe two or three other vehicles, assuredly pickup trucks. The main
service station in Malta has a pile of tires out back equal in size to the
garage. Most of them look as if they exploded, as did mine, not yet a
month old. The mechanic says all are evidence that a lot of people are
dumb enough to drive the Breaks without six-ply truck tires. The sharp
gravel slices tires, but at 55 on rough gravel, the driver often doesn't
notice until the tire is a tangle of smelly rubber and ripped threads.
Best to carry two spares.

And best to be ready to be stranded. A sudden thunderstorm turns
some of the roads to sticky "gumbo" mud. Impossible to drive on it,

even for the most able of four-by-fours. Tires snowball in gumbo until they are double in size, then they spin out. Best to stay put for a couple of days until the roads dry. Never mind if you have an appointment or a plane to catch. You can't get there from here, at least not today. This situation must have been even more difficult in the 1970s, before behemoth diesel pickups and reliable truck tires. Then, the tailend of the Breaks must have seemed closer to the era of wolfers and horse thieves than to our own time. It was closer then, at least in appearance, than in most other times between the 1960s and the time of wolfers and horse thieves.

Breaks is a cracker-barrel term for the edge of the plains. Lying below that edge is a series of long, down-trending ridges and gullies, erosional features cut by glacial melt from the Rockies a couple of hundred miles west. Once the Missouri was massive here, and it still is a major river, but it seems a mere stream resting at the bottom of the channel cut by its former Pleistocene self.

Between the time of the horse thieves and the 1960s, this broad, broken valley was in fact the most populous section of the Breaks. River bottoms had year-round water and good soil so became the hubs of population that John Wesley Powell predicted. Ferries crossed the river, and thriving little towns lay on both sides of it, with general stores, freight offices, and a couple of dance halls that are still recalled fondly by some of Malta's most senior of citizens. Now only a broken-down cabin remains here and there, a rusting old harrow, a settler's midden, or a disappearing foundation claimed by rabbits. The land along the river bottom began returning to what it was when the New Deal moved the people away, but not as part of Henry Lantz's resettlement scheme. These were irrigated lands and the most productive. Most of the farmers could make a go of it here. Resettlement applied to the flat-baked plains above, not to this river bottom.

A scheme of far grander proportions moved the bottomland farmers away. Before the Depression, this was a stretch of farms and ranches; then one day, ten thousand men and their camp followers descended and built what was a wonder of the world, a dam across the Missouri that was at the time the largest earth-filled impoundment ever built, larger than the next closest by a factor of six. In the interests of protecting people from floods and employing the destitute, FDR's minions commissioned this monster, ensnared a hulking river, and moved the people out. The construction of Fort Peck Dam created a near-geologic-scale rumble in the social and natural history of Montana. Yet in 1976, when Mike Hedrick, a young biologist, made the drive south out of Malta to an area of the Breaks called the UL Bend, the place was so empty it seemed to have been that way forever. And on any reasonable scale of forever, it has been.

Yet Hedrick was driving not off the edge of the world but into the very center of a part of it. He drove into a pivot point, a flash point. Here, humanity's relationship with the natural world has evolved along a central and defining contradiction. In many ways this contradiction, this dichotomy, this irresolvable battle with ourselves provided the creative tension that has moved conservation forward, not just in the Breaks, but nationwide. And has moved it backward and backward and backward, so that its issues are no more resolved in our time than in the 1970s or in the day of Theodore Roosevelt, the man who best embodied this deep dichotomy. And yet, they must be resolved if our species is to have the slightest chance of not fouling our nest so badly that we find continuation of life as we know it impossible, assuming we have not already done so. The news of each passing day makes this resolution a taller and taller assumption. I am drawn to the Breaks because their harsh and misanthropic rules make possible at least the contemplation of such a resolution.

✍

The founding philosophy of conservation had to have been the furthest thought from Hedrick's mind when he made that dusty drive. Not that he is not capable of deep thought. His whole career as a wildlife biologist in federal employ rode the sharp edge of this conflict from one end to the other, and he's plenty smart enough and reflective enough, at least when I talked to him about this late in his career, a year before his retirement, to fathom every bit of this better than I can.

Then, though, he was a young man out to do a job. Raised on a ranch in Washington, he was no stranger to big, empty country but had learned from even his earliest years that the prairie is not at all empty of wildlife, if one knows how to look. So he looked and finally trained formally as a biologist and then signed on with the Fish and Wildlife Service. That early job in the Breaks meant he and his wife were to drive off the edge of the world and live for a while in a cabin at UL Bend, today a designated wilderness within the Charles M. Russell National Wildlife Refuge. His assignment was to plan an engineered duck farm.

The refuge was then a new entity, formally designated as such in 1963 by the Department of the Interior. That designation was intended as a transition for a parcel of property set aside during the Depression, 1.1 million acres of land bought by the feds for Fort Peck Dam's backwaters but never flooded. The social engineers of the New Deal may well have been prepared to take down whole rivers and whole communities with their dams, but within all this was a seminal and genuine streak of conservation greater than that of any other administration. FDR wanted that million acres set aside for conservation. Wrangling with the ranchers and their representatives in Congress about grazing rights on the refuge kept the matter bottled up until the 1980s. This wrangling spanned the period of political ascendancy of the ranching interests, when the lobby was reworking the Taylor Grazing Act to its own purposes. Stalling a refuge for nearly fifty years was, for this lobby, a trivial matter.

A compromise of sorts arose in the 1930s when the refuge was first set aside, with the ranchers winning the rights to graze their cattle on it. Never mind that every bit of the wildlife depends on the grass the cattle consume. And never mind that the Department of the Interior's 1963 document establishing the refuge lays out its purpose in black type over white space: to restore bison to their native range. To date, more than forty years later, no progress has been made on that front. This is not so say no progress has been made period. The refuge was in a state of struggle from the beginning, and although it would be difficult to imagine that Hedrick could have foreseen his career-long relationship with it when he first made the forlorn trip into the Breaks, he would ride point on the struggle over the refuge until he retired in 2005.

Hedrick's task on that first assignment was to prepare the way for yet another massive rearrangement of the hydraulics of the Breaks. The issue here has always been aridity, so attempts to reengineer the land-scape for more water—whether for raising cattle or for the manipu-lation of wildlife—have developed from a singular mindset.

In the mid-1970s, the federal government through its Fish and Wildlife Service proposed to snake a long, high-voltage transmission line from the power grid south about sixty miles to the Missouri River. This line would power massive pumps that would lift water from the Missouri to flood a bench just above the river, land that used to be farmers' fields. The resulting artificial wetland, in a near desert, would become a duck farm. The narrow explanation for this enterprise is that the Fish and Wildlife Service has drawn a great deal of its revenue from stamp permits that waterfowl hunters buy, allowing them to shoot mi-gratory ducks and geese. By law, the service was to use the stamp rev-enue to create more habitat to support more ducks so that more hunters would buy more stamps. Never mind natural conditions. This arrange-ment went so far as to put the service in the business of controlling predators, which it did then and does now, trapping and killing car-nivores that prey on ducks, such as skunks and raccoons, just as ranch-ers have their animal damage control.

The Fish and Wildlife Service's role in this stems from the messy birth process of the conservation movement beginning with Theodore Roosevelt. In a battle with states, the federal government won the right to set bag limits on migratory waterfowl. It was then regarded as a victory for conservationists, but then and now we can ask, Which conservationists?

Certainly Hedrick did not agree with his assignment; in fact, he openly opposed the plan. In the 1970s, maybe even especially then, biologists had a growing sense that the narrow focus of wildlife biology on hunted species had done a great disservice to wildlife in general. Today, that spot in the refuge is bone dry, covered from one end to the other with prairie dog towns, and is one of the few sites in the world to harbor the extremely endangered black-footed ferret. A battle was won, but the war continues, though more quietly now. In the beginning it raged, pitting the scions of the conservation movement against one another in vituperative battles typical of any civil war. Theodore Roosevelt, certainly, but Gifford Pinchot, George Bird Grinnell, William Hornaday, Aldo Leopold, Bob Marshall, Franklin Roosevelt, Rexford Tugwell, and especially Harold Ickes would all fire shots in an ugly screaming match, still unresolved.

Ducks were not at all a trivial matter in the 1920s. Congress had before it a bill that would create the duck stamp and mark the revenue for buying waterfowl habitat. This triggered a fight with states that were themselves deriving considerable revenue from a sort of conservation tragedy of the aerial commons. Ducks and geese are migratory, so they fly over and stop off in many states along their flyways. It was in the interest of any given state to let its hunters shoot as many of the ducks as possible, thereby attracting more hunters and taking the revenue from their license fees. Gun and ammunition manufacturers also had a stake in seeing as many shots fired as possible, and the number possible then was considerable. In 1929, a hunter could legally kill twenty-five ducks a day using methods such as baited feeding fields and automatic shotguns. The hunting season of a hundred days theoretically allowed a hunter twenty-five hundred ducks per year.

Not surprisingly, waterfowl populations were then in serious trouble, slammed between this slaughter and the unprecedented destruction of prairie habitat by plows. Biologists estimated that the numbers had dropped from a billion in 1870, to one hundred million in 1930, and, more precipitously, to twenty million by 1934. At that low point in 1934, if seven million duck hunters had bought licenses and each hunter had shot three ducks—never mind the twenty-five the law allowed—the birds would have disappeared.

There was, as is almost always the case in conservation, a class overlay on this. During the Depression game animals came under increasing pressure from hungry rural people. Biologists in the Breaks report, as one might expect, that deer, antelope, and elk numbers reached an all-time nadir during the region's most desperate years. Congress's proposal to create wildfowl refuges included a measure that would have allowed public shooting grounds on those refuges, a measure opposed by private shooting clubs for the wealthy. In addition, there was a bureaucratic overlay; the Forest Service was fighting the possibility that any other federal agency might get any other federal land for these wildlife refuges. Irving Brant was a journalist who walked rather naively into this fray. He recalls in his memoir that he and an idealistic colleague, Willard Van Name, "were sentimental interlopers in a pro-hunting, pro-lumbering, pro-power, anti-park gathering [a federal hearing] stacked in advance and stage-managed by the Forest Service."[1]

All of this was about a lot more than ducks. Go back just a generation before to that wood-paneled club in Manhattan where a young Theodore Roosevelt helped found the American Bison Society and later the Boone and Crockett Club. Note that the room is literally filled with wealthy hunters, who are acting primarily to preserve a "bully" sort of wilderness experience for their class. Note the presence of Gifford Pinchot, but also George Bird Grinnell, the biologist who about thirty years before had gotten off a boat at Rocky Point in the Missouri Breaks and compiled one of the first biological surveys of the northern plains. Also note the presence of William Hornaday, curator of the New York Zoological Garden. Just a few years earlier, Hornaday had heard that the last remnants of wild bison were to be found in Montana just southeast of the Breaks, so he mounted an expedition in 1886, searched long and hard, and finally found a bison, which he shot and had stuffed for exhibition in New York. Both Hornaday and Grinnell were on record as believing that the extermination of the bison was inevitable and not such a bad thing. Hornaday did help establish bison preserves, but his racism had kept him from obtaining those animals from an Indian-controlled herd in Montana. Finally, note the presence in that room of Andrew Carnegie, the industrialist.

Also in the room was an unresolved conflict best marked with a story Pinchot told. If an inverse Pinchot existed in a parallel universe, it would be John Muir, the reclusive naturalist who believed above all in wilderness for the sake of wilderness and preferred hermetic mountain travels to bureaucratic squabbling. Strangely, the two men had met and spent time together on a trip through the Grand Canyon. Much of the American conservation movement could probably have been foretold in conversations that occurred during their time together, but we don't have a complete record of it. We do have a telling detail reported by Pinchot: The two men had stumbled on a tarantula. Pinchot said somewhat incredulously, "Muir wouldn't let me kill it. He said it had as much right to be there as we did."[2]

This central contradiction and all its layers played out in the duck issue twenty years later, and it is a mark of the unresolved conflict of TR's time that a couple of his pivotal allies were bitter opponents in that later issue. This battle over ducks also stands as one of the more sordid but telling anecdotes of conservation history.

Grinnell, true to his middle name, had also conceived of and founded the first incarnation of the American Audubon Society in 1886. That group, established then and still functioning as the protector of all things avian, was, for a time, simply bought off by the gun manufacturers. The gunmakers in 1911 had given the fledgling group $125,000 in five installments, no strings attached, other than, as Brant reports, that the salary of its director, T. Gilbert Pearson, was to be doubled. Pearson later weighed in against imposing bag limits on ducks, arguing that this was an ethical question "each sportsman . . . must decide for himself."[3] This was also, not coincidentally, the position of the gunmakers. Pearson's ally in this was George Bird Grinnell, an even more enthusiastic acceptor of gun company money. Their opponent was William Hornaday, who helped whip up a firestorm within Audubon that eventually became a struggle for its soul, a grass-roots effort to purge the leadership, an effort eventually successful.

This was more than an internecine struggle; it was evidence of a conservation movement trying to define itself, to evolve to match the values of a rapidly evolving industrial society. These people—Grinnell, Hornaday, Pinchot, Muir—had personally witnessed an era of horrible destruction of wildlife at the hands of industrialism, just as they had witnessed an unprecedented creation of wealth by the same force. This evolution was but a subset of a general upheaval in politics, and the larger battle, although framed in terms of Progressivism, not conservation, still involved some of the same players. Not the least of these was a thoroughly urban politico schooled by the hard-knuckled politics of Chicago. Harold Ickes would emerge from this industrial setting to become, according to his biographer, T. H. Watkins, one of three secretaries of the interior in our nation's history who viscerally understood the value of wilderness.

A poor boy raised in an industrial town in Pennsylvania, Ickes moved to Chicago as a young man and worked his way into an education and then into Chicago's politics as a reform Republican. He was an ardent supporter of Theodore Roosevelt, which is to say a Progressive. By the end of Roosevelt's first term, Ickes had risen to some national prominence in the party and was positioned for a key role at a key moment in Progressive politics. He allied with two Progressive activists, Amos Pinchot (Gifford Pinchot's brother) and William Allen White, the Kansas newspaperman who became the voice of the Progressives.

Ickes personally accompanied Roosevelt on the train from New York to Chicago for the riotous Republican National Convention of 1912, a gathering marked by fistfights. The Progressives later learned that the forces of nominee William Taft had protected the convention's podium with barbed wire concealed in bunting.

Taft's mainstream prevailed, causing the Progressives to bolt the party and back TR's presidential bid, fronted by his Bull Moose Party. That, of course, failed but served to energize the Progressive movement and separate it from Republican control. That energy remained for Franklin Roosevelt to tap later. One of the chief political assets handed from Roosevelt to Roosevelt was Ickes, whom the latter Roosevelt immediately appointed as his secretary of the interior when he was elected. Ickes held the post throughout FDR's tenure.

Yet incubating within this Progressive movement was another split. The Progressives had formed and were united by Theodore Roosevelt's zeal for reform and trust busting. As we have seen, much of his founding of the conservation movement grew from that zeal. Public lands were counterbalances to the corporate control of lands. Conservation was to protect watersheds and forests to benefit yeomen farmers and independent communities. That is, the conservation of Pinchot and Theodore Roosevelt was very much utilitarian. At this point, no serious political circles had room for wilderness cranks like John Muir, who was mostly regarded as a curiosity, a tarantula hugger.

This is the larger political backdrop for such events as the fight over the integrity of the Audubon Society. The issue involved more than bag limits. At stake was the role of wildlife in American life. Did wildlife exist simply to provide income for gun manufacturers and sport for wealthy elitist hunters like Teddy Roosevelt, or did wildlife and wild things have a claim to existence independent of utility? In these early years, the demarcation between these positions was not cleanly drawn, nor is it today. Thus, combatants often popped up on different sides in different debates, depending on the issue, which continues to be the case.

✍

Franklin Roosevelt set out to defeat the Great Depression with an exercise he called "pump priming," an apt metaphor in that it involved a great deal of water. And, conversely, the lack of a great deal of water. The goal of this exercise was putting people to work with projects large and small; *leaf raking* was the derogatory term. Indeed, as we have seen, some were as nonsensical as the project to build a brand new recreation center for a town and then depopulating that town with a subsequent project. No one said the projects needed to be useful or logical, but they did have to put people to work in those places suffering the worst effects of the Depression. The Dust Bowl and farm crises made the need greatest in the West, especially on the plains, but this need combined with other factors to shape the nature of that work.

First, the West held most of the nation's public lands, especially forest reserves. The rising concern for conservation allowed the administration to put a lot of men and women to work on these public lands, building trails and campgrounds and fighting erosion and fires. To this day, the public's use of the West's forests and parks relies on facilities built by the Civilian Conservation Corps.

Second, the West is also defined by its lack of water, the aridity that left lands unoccupied and public in the first place. The pond-for-every-farm mentality of the administration caused the New Dealers to manipulate water in far more grandiose schemes than simply ponds. Dams became an irresistible draw for the New Dealers. Dams are relatively simple and easy to plan, easy to replicate, and they employ huge numbers of pick-and-shovel laborers. Just as enticingly to the New Dealers, dams were at the time viewed as progressive. The model was the Tennessee Valley Authority, an enormous public works project built to generate electricity for public use. Federal dams remove control of power bills from corporations. They have socialized power and busted monopolies.

Conservation was probably very far from Harold Ickes's mind when he began his new assignment at the Interior. What had to be foremost on his mind was an all-consuming struggle for power—political, economic, and electric—in which his department dominated as the designated head of the Public Works Administration. The Interior handled the money that would build the massive system of Depression-era dams on the West's major rivers, the Colorado and the Columbia, but would also control the purse strings on everything from sewer systems to the construction of new post offices and courthouses. Ickes came to office with the charge of spending $3.3 billion as rapidly as possible at a time when, by his own admission, he couldn't comprehend how much money that was.

We have already seen how an administration, desperate for fully formed plans, seized on the ideas of Henry Lantz to build a major New Deal program. The New Dealers wanted projects that could make shovels fly today, not spend years on an engineer's drawing board. Oddly enough, another such idea was languishing in the Missouri Breaks, a plan all ready to go. The irrigation schemes fostered by the first Roosevelt's Reclamation Act almost immediately produced projects on the Milk River just north of the Breaks. As part of that work, engineers during the Calvin Coolidge administration had identified a project that simply dwarfed anything yet imagined on the Milk, a tributary of the much larger Missouri.

Dreams of damming the Missouri River at an Indian trading post called Fort Peck, however, predated even Theodore Roosevelt's scheme for watering the West. One of the principals in the trading post, Colonel Campbell Kennedy Peck, reportedly traveled to Washington DC in 1879 to propose a dam at the site of his store. His argument was that it would aid river navigation by controlling downstream flows, and, at the time, his operation depended on its river link. Nothing came of Peck's plan, but oddly his name would still attach to the dam he had envisioned when the New Dealers finally built it.

Despite Peck's earlier disappointment, some serious discussions about the dam did precede the New Deal. A series of surveys that had begun in 1890 finally led to more surveys and the Flood Control Act of 1927. In 1932, a month before Franklin Roosevelt's election, two officials of the Army Corps of Engineers toured the site with Leo Coleman, the mayor of the town of Glasgow, and Sam Rugg, who headed the town's chamber of commerce. The local paper reported the excursion and quoted Coleman's words on viewing the eight-thousand-foot-wide valley where the dam was to be located: "My God, man, it would cost a million dollars to build a dam across there!"[4]

It was actually slated to cost more like $160 million, which was fine with the New Dealers. That money would put ten thousand men to work, and that was exactly the point. More money meant more men working, so more was better. The dam site is in Valley County, where, in 1931, at least half of the farmers needed some sort of relief. The Red Cross, providing the only relief in the Hoover years, was by then overwhelmed and responding to only the most desperate cases, but it *was* responding in Valley County. It was distributing food, coal, and even feed for livestock throughout 1932. The welfare of Valley County, however, was not the point. The dam project drew workers from throughout Montana, a shift of seismic proportions in the labor force, still readable today in many family histories. When I ordered some research material on Fort Peck from the University of Montana's library in Missoula, even at today's speeds a hard seven-hour drive from Fort Peck, the twenty-something librarian began recounting how his family history had been rearranged by a series of relatives who worked on the dam.

Furthermore, the effects were not limited to Montana. In 1934, the Malta newspaper reported that a tent city of 150 people had sprung up in a city park. All were there looking for jobs as rock pickers on the dam. "The types of traveling means are to be noticed. Some have their goods and equipment loaded onto trucks, others have trailers loaded with their belongings. One trailer had a house built on it, a truly elaborate screened-in affair," the paper reported.[5] The tent dwellers had come from North Dakota, Missouri, Kansas, Nebraska, and Nevada. These northern-tier Joads were drawn to an enterprise that was truly heroic, an engineering feat pulled off by the sweat of ordinary people, the very essence of New Deal mythology and sufficient to bring Roosevelt himself for two visits to the dam. The project would eventually draw a peak workforce of 10,456, mostly men. Wages were fifty cents an hour, eighty cents for a foreman, about double the wage for any other job that might be found in the area.

From the beginning, engineers were never sure the structure could be built at all. It was simply the largest, by far, of any earth-filled dam attempted. The largest before had been the Gatun Dam, completed by the Army Corps in 1912 in Panama. Fort Peck's design called for more than five times as much fill as in the dam in Panama, to be dredged from the river bottom and pumped into the structure's concrete shell. Even the machinery to build such a dam was unprecedented; shipbuilders were among the first workers on-site, and they built four specially designed 12,500-horsepower electric dredges.

The rationale for all this work, other than creating paychecks, was less clear. The stated purpose for the dam was the same imagined by Colonel Peck, controlling the river for navigation. Backers, however, Christmas-treed this rationale, adding erosion control, electricity production, flood control. Several of these, specifically the production of electricity and control of floods, were incompatible, in that they required the release of water at different times. One set of historians who reviewed the Army Corps' rationale concluded that "Fort Peck Dam and Reservoir would not have been built had circumstances been normal (i.e. no depression)."[6] It was leaf raking writ large.

Even before Roosevelt took office, Montana's congressional delegation had begun lobbying for Fort Peck on the grounds that it could generate electricity to power mines in western Montana, then modernizing to use electrical equipment. Specifically, Senator Burton K. Wheeler, the powerful Montana Democrat, took up the cause. He and the rest of the political muscle of the state went to work even before the Army Corps had finished tests establishing the dam's feasibility. The politicos were not the only ones to jump the gun. The Army Corps itself approved and funded the project before that testing of feasibility was completed. The corps then dropped electrical generation from the dam's design, and Congress, including Wheeler, electricity's champion, accepted the change. The dam eventually did get generators, but not until the run-up to World War II. Today, it is mostly justified for making navigation easier on the Missouri. Barge traffic now carries not trading post supplies but wheat.

The costs of the dam ultimately amounted to a lot more than $160 million. The dam is located not in mountains but on relatively flat land, meaning that it has to flood an enormous area to store a significant amount of water. At full pool, the reservoir extends upstream 180 miles and is 16 miles wide at its extreme. The meandering shoreline of the pool stretches to 1,500 miles. It floods about 250,000 acres, which were river-bottom land, the most easily irrigated and the most productive. So while Lantz and his minions were on the prairies buying up bankrupt dry farms, a parallel crew was at work in the bottoms buying up about a hundred viable farms and ranches. Long-settled communities in the Breaks simply disappeared, almost overnight. Broke dryland farmers and flooded-out bottomland farmers alike went to work for dam wages.

❧

When Boulder Dam, now Hoover Dam, was completed in 1935 on the Arizona-Nevada state line, Harold Ickes was granted the first speech of the day, and he said, "Here behind this massive dam is slowly accumulating a rich deposit of wealth greater than all the mines of the West have ever produced, wealth to be drawn upon for all the time to come for the renewed life and continued benefit of generations of Americans."[7] Utility was the guiding hand of arguably the most ambitious program of river rearrangement in history. Yet to label Ickes a utilitarian would be a mistake, just as it would be to do so with all of the New Dealers in general. The dam building did indeed flow straight from the heart of the New Deal's utilitarian side. The more ardent among them could express this vein in terminology rivaling the most florid of the socialist realists. For instance, this from David Lilienthal:

> Today it is builders and technicians we turn to, men armed not with the ax and rifle and bowie knife, but with the Diesel engine, the bulldozer, the giant electric shovel, the retort—and most of all with an emerging kind of skill, a modern knack of organization and execution. When these men have imagination and faith, they can move mountains; out of their skills they can create new jobs, relieve human drudgery, give new life and fruitfulness to worn out lands, put yokes upon the streams, and transmit the minerals of the earth and the plants of the fields into machines of wizardry to spin out the stuff of a way of life new to this world.[8]

This was indeed the dominant strain of the New Deal, but there was a counterpoint, and that too became a legacy. In the beginning this counterpoint was a barely audible "movement for the unqualified preservation of land and wildlife," a "kind of fifth column," according to Watkins, "incoherent and shattered into factions outside the government."[9] This situation was more than just happenstance. The conservation movement itself was fractured and mired in the bitter politics pushed by Pinchot's messianic zeal. It is the greatest irony, then, that the movement toward wilderness preservation began within Pinchot's Forest Service with Bob Marshall, Aldo Leopold, and Arthur Carhart, a landscape architect working on parks. Both Leopold and Marshall were, by the beginning of the 1930s, actively engaged in promoting the cause of wilderness for its own sake. In 1935, the pair, along with some sympathizers, founded the Wilderness Society. Marshall's boss by then was Harold Ickes. Early on, Marshall had expressed support for Ickes's controversial choice of commissioner of the Bureau of Indian Affairs, John Collier, so Collier in turn appointed Marshall head of forestry for the bureau, which moved him from the Forest Service to the Department of the Interior. The move allowed Ickes, who was sympathetic to Marshall's views on wilderness, to protect the increasingly controversial Marshall. Ickes, ostensibly the utilitarian, sheltered a belief in wilderness for its own sake, the very antithesis of utilitarianism. Watkins wrote, "The relationship between the young forester and the Secretary . . . would never reach the level of what could be called friendship, but one in which the two men shared—however unlikely such an alliance may have appeared on the surface—a common love of wilderness."[10]

Moves such as Marshall's assignment, though, also served to give wilderness a real voice in the administration, a voice that FDR, a self-proclaimed conservationist, was inclined to hear. Ickes himself began a program of actively promoting national parks and even opposed further road building in some parks, a move that went directly against the grain of the bulldozer-and-shovel theme of the New Deal.

The contradiction inherent in this opposition broke to the surface when Ickes proposed the creation of a department of conservation. The main thrust of that would, of course, be the relocation of the Forest Service itself from the Agriculture Department to the Interior. This would have a greater effect than Marshall's bureaucratic shuffle from the service to the Interior; it would lessen the Forest Service's utilitarian spin, making conservation its chief goal. By then, the Forest Service was firmly controlled by the timber industry, creating a bureaucratic inertia that was decidedly pro-development. This pro-development bias played out in some very real ways. For instance, a major dustup of the era was a nasty battle over Olympic National Park, in Washington, which Ickes wanted to enlarge dramatically for preservation by attaching Forest Service lands to it. The Forest Service opposed him, mouthing lines taken straight from the timber industry. Ickes won that one. Ickes, however, lost a second key battle, one that was remarkably prescient. He proposed a wilderness act, prefiguring the landmark legislation of 1964 that finally made wilderness for the sake of wilderness into federal law. He was a generation ahead of his time.

Nonetheless, Ickes maintained firm control of the National Park Service, which had been a part of the Department of the Interior from its inception. He used it to preside over what was the most expansive period in the service's history. He waged battle upon battle for expansion and won, creating Kings Canyon, Olympic, Isle Royale, Organ Pipe Cactus, Great Smoky Mountains, Shenandoah, and Grand Teton national parks and Cape Hatteras National Seashore. During the first seven years of his tenure, the national parks system grew from eight million acres to more than twenty million. And quietly, he added wildlife refuges, many of them carved out of lands acquired by resettlement, and one in particular carved from land the government had bought for Fort Peck Dam, the 1.1 million acres that was to become the Charles M. Russell National Wildlife Refuge. In 1935, Ickes's Department of the Interior sent the renowned biologist Olaus Murie to survey what was then being called the Fort Peck Migratory Bird Refuge, a designation that Roosevelt wanted as a part of the dam's legacy. In 1936, he signed the executive order creating the refuge under that name, but it was then a refuge in name only and not even with the name it would eventually bear. It became instead a legal battleground for the next fifty years—fifty—with the lines pitched along the very contradictions that dominated the New Deal.

Again, Roosevelt ruled using creative tension, by allowing contradictory views within his administration. His people were not "yes" men but hired to do combat for ideas. Those unresolved contradictions outlived FDR. At what would become the Charles M. Russell National Wildlife Refuge, the contradictory style of management actually became formalized. The refuge was placed under dual management by two very different agencies constantly at odds, sharing only the organizational mark that both were within the Department of the Interior.

⌘

It's a measure of the Russell Wildlife Refuge's tortured history that it was formally established three times and even after the third time in 1976 could not work toward its primary goal, the protection of wildlife, until a round of court battles ended ten years later. In setting aside the refuge, FDR's administration placed it under the joint management of the new Grazing Service and the Fish and Wildlife Service. By then, though, the Grazing Service was on its way to being dominated by ranchers, a process more or less accomplished by 1946, when it combined with the old General Land Office to become the Bureau of Land Management, also a creature of the Department of the Interior. The BLM superintends all of the unhomesteaded lands along with most of the lands bought back by the federal government during the New Deal. The exception is the National Grasslands, also bought back by the government but charged to the Agriculture Department's Forest Service as spoils of the tug of war between that service and the BLM. Historically, the BLM has been not so much a land management agency as a grazing agency, with its direction set by the grazing district boards made up of ranchers. The BLM began exercising its power over the Russell Wildlife Refuge from its beginning. From the start, the Russell Wildlife Refuge was a grazing refuge. Roosevelt's order creating the refuge allowed this.

In the 1930s, there was a great deal of concern over the survival of certain game species, largely because local residents, trying to survive the deprivations of the Depression, had killed so many game animals that their numbers were now meager. Therefore, Roosevelt's order identified two "primary species" for conservation: the pronghorn antelope and the sharp-tailed grouse. It specified that management provide maximum forage for those two, and allowed the killing of other "nonpredatory" species of wildlife, but said, "In no case shall the consumption of forage by the combined population of the wildlife species be allowed to increase the burden of the range dedicated to the primary species."[11] Any modern biologist would recognize this directive as not only unsound ecologically but also not really manageable. That's the biologist's dilemma, but it gets worse. The order added: "All forage resources within this range or preserve shall be available, except as herein otherwise provided with respect to wildlife, for domestic livestock."

Perhaps recognizing the impossibility of the task, the administration did not even appoint a refuge superintendent until 1940, and only fourteen years after that was the first survey of range conditions finished. The wildlife refuge's management acknowledges this standoff in its official history: "Even though the 1954 range survey was conducted cooperatively by the BLM and FWS, wildlife interests clearly were secondary to livestock. This one fact typified the entire forty year period of dual administration by the BLM and FWS. The divergent philosophies and basic objectives of the two agencies were inequitable, and wildlife and their habitats continued to deteriorate."[12]

Pressure to settle this began percolating within the Interior Department itself and surfaced in 1963 with a time-honored bureaucratic solution to a problem of substance: rebranding. The Interior changed the name of the game range to the "Charles M. Russell National Wildlife Range." With that change, however, came a new management document laying out the goals of the range, and those goals came down on the side of wildlife. The document specifically admits the fundamental problem: "Years of excessive grazing have depleted vegetative cover, reduced stands of more palatable perennial grasses and allowed increases of less desirable weeds and shrubs."[13] The plan specifically spells out the protection of wildlife as the range's primary purpose and goes so far as to explicitly call for restoration of bison and bighorn sheep to their native range. (The bighorn sheep are indeed back but not the bison.) The document also signals that the department was coming to grips with what was, in the early 1960s, a growing awareness of the plight of some species, specifying that a major goal was "to preserve the following endangered and vanishing species: The mountain plover, upland plover, long-billed curlew, burrowing owl, bald eagle, golden eagles, mountain bluebird, black-footed ferret, black-tailed prairie dog, kit fox and wolverine." This was ten years before passage of the Endangered Species Act.

The document—then labeled a proposal—was signed by secretary of the interior Stuart Udall, one of the three secretaries who, along with Ickes before and Cecil Andrus after, had a visceral appreciation for the value of wilderness. No one seemed concerned, however, that the man in charge of both the BLM and the Fish and Wildlife Service had laid out a directive for wildlife. Says the official history supplied by the service: "By that time the problem of joint administration began to be apparent at the Washington level. Several attempts to realign management back in favor of wildlife through Secretarial policy memos and cooperative agreements between the agencies failed to resolve the basic problems."[14]

That is to say, the grazing boards were so firmly in control of the BLM that even the nominal boss of the Department of the Interior couldn't enforce his own sincerely felt directive to protect wildlife. It was a Republican administration that finally tried to resolve the structural contradiction. Richard Nixon's interior secretary, Rogers Morton, attempted to deal with the problem at the Russell Wildlife Refuge and parallel fights at four other national refuges by dicing up the baby. He assigned two of those to the Fish and Wildlife Service and the other three, including the Russell, to the BLM. This move so angered environmentalists that they exercised their then-considerable political muscle in Congress, which in 1976 passed legislation giving management of all five to the Fish and Wildlife Service, along with a directive that the land be managed for wildlife.

The Fish and Wildlife Service set out to enforce the legislation, so the cattlemen sued. A federal district judge sided with the cattlemen, ruling against the Department of the Interior, by then headed by the notorious James Watt. Watt, not surprisingly, decided not to contest the judge's ruling against his agency, but environmental groups, especially the National Wildlife Federation, had earlier and fortuitously intervened in the case. The federation appealed to the Ninth Circuit Court of Appeals and won. In 1985, almost fifty years after its creation as a wildlife refuge, the Russell was granted the legal footing it needed to protect wildlife.

∽

Mike Hedrick sits in his office in Lewistown, Montana, still looking as if he just stepped off the ranch. But he did that a long time ago, leaving his family's ranch in eastern Washington after high school to take degrees in range management and wildlife biology, two fields that represent the primary opposing forces of the grassland West. Hedrick still looks the part of a rancher—boots, jeans, hat, squint, and wrinkles of a lifelong plainsman—but he calls himself a wildlife biologist, primarily a big-game biologist.

His first job after school was with the Bureau of Land Management, rounding up wild horses in Nevada, a management policy that has been a contentious issue. (Feral horses wipe out forage for both wildlife and cattle, although many feel they deserve protection themselves.) But he left the BLM simply because it was then (and continues to be to a lesser extent today) the captive of ranchers, and he joined the Fish and Wildlife Service for the remainder of his career. His first FWS posting was at the UL Bend in the Russell Wildlife Refuge, where he and the rest of the refuge staff faced down the duck farm proposal. That is, he was front and center in the two struggles that would come to dominate his career throughout: grazing rights and the battle over ducks.

He explained what the situation was with both the BLM and the Forest Service at the start of his career: "Those agencies were then and still are dominated by commodity interests, be it timber, mining, or grazing."[15] That is an unusually blunt statement for a bureaucrat, the sort of statement that makes a land manager a lightning rod, but Hedrick made it clear he didn't mind being quoted. He was looking ahead to retirement. "By the time this comes out, it will be a moot point," he said.

The timing of his move to the Russell Wildlife Refuge put him right on the edge of change: the 1976 act of Congress to shift full responsibility for the refuge to the Fish and Wildlife Service. From that day, the service began removing cows. It leased grazing rights under a different philosophy: cattle could graze as a tool, which is often a legitimate one. The plants of the plains have coevolved with grazing by such animals as bison and elk. Removing that grazing and losing its effects can often actually damage the landscape, and virtually nowhere are there enough elk or bison to get the job done. Carefully managed grazing can indeed be an effective tool, but historically the refuge and surrounding lands had been grazed by cattle well beyond the point of careful management. The BLM land still is.

The Fish and Wildlife Service operates under a different law as well as a different philosophy from those of the BLM. It can charge market rate for grazing leases, not the steeply subsidized rates of the BLM. Further, when a ranch changes ownership, the service can retire the lease. It also can refuse to provide "improvements," such as ponds and corrals, which ranchers view as an entitlement on BLM lands. These measures took time to kick into gear in the Russell Wildlife Refuge, especially with the ten years of legal battles that ended with the Ninth Circuit Court decision. In the meantime, Hedrick took an assignment in Alaska but returned to the Russell in 1995 to become its manager. The net result of all this on the refuge is easily measured. When the FWS took over in 1976, about eighty thousand cow-calf pairs were grazed there. By the time Hedrick retired in 2005, that number had been cut to about twenty-five thousand.

The effects have been particularly dramatic. One of the first places to become cow free was an area north of the UL Bend, managed for wilderness for almost all of the thirty years since Hedrick first went there. The border between that area and adjacent BLM lands is visible in satellite imagery, so dramatic are grazing's effects on the landscape. Meanwhile, some of the very ranchers who engaged in this long struggle with the Fish and Wildlife Service used almost exactly the same phrase in a series of interviews when I asked them about this issue. "We see the handwriting on the wall," they said, by which they mean wildlife has won the battle for the refuge, and it may be time for them, the ranchers, to move on. Hedrick is not their favorite person.

In a sense, though, the second struggle that spanned his career, the one that began with the battle over ducks, is more crucial to conservation than this grazing issue. He acknowledges that his agency, despite being strongly oriented toward wildlife, was dominated in the early days by single-species management. This is the utilitarian side of conservation: that nature exists to produce commodities—timber and grass or elk and ducks—and it is a manager's job to run the landscape like a farm to maximize the production of the target species. Yet it is misleading to call this utilitarianism. It is simply wrong in a practical sense. Biologists in the twentieth century began learning what some of the more visionary of their numbers had begun preaching early in the century: that an ecosystem is a whole, a web of interlocking parts. The whole is greater than the sum of the parts. The members of an ecosystem provide services for one another, so that the survival of each depends on the integrity of the whole. Wolves are not the enemy of elk and deer but the counterbalance to their excesses.

The realization of the power of this notion dawned slowly, and in some corners of the bureaucratic world it has not dawned at all. For Hedrick, the dawning began with the duck farm. "We would have taken all that sage grouse–pronghorn–prairie dog–black-footed ferret habitat and flooded it for mallards and pintails," he said. "I thought, what do we have more of on the landscape? Waterfowl are common, still real common, yet the things we were going to eradicate with our tinkering were becoming much less common."

By then, the Fish and Wildlife Service had set up an ecological services division. "They recognized sooner than most refuge folks that the era of single-species management was going to have to come to an end. We were losing the wildlife that we had taken for granted. . . . We were losing that across the landscape. . . . That was, of course, what people like Leopold and others told us in the '30s, but I didn't see it becoming really common management practice until the late '70s, early '80s."

Biological education changed, and young people with new ideas were hired into land management agencies, and an evolution in thought occurred. That very transition is also happening in the BLM and in Gifford Pinchot's Forest Service, an evolution that no doubt has him spinning in his grave.

It is said that science advances one funeral at a time.

Ten

A LEARNED LEGACY

Ranchers have been stereotyped to be the bad guys. If it weren't for ranchers, then who knows what that country would be like now. Basically it's the same as it's always been.

—*Breaks rancher Ross Wiederrick*

A drive into the Breaks at certain times of the year has the edge of adventure. I jumped the season once, slogging my way south through the deserted landscape just when a warm spell was demolishing the drifts of a late-winter storm. Any water turns the usual hardpan clay surface into the region's storied gumbo mud. Such events can leave one trapped in the place for days while waiting for roads to dry. The land has a way of holding on to you, or as the locals put it, "If you stick to the land when it's dry, it'll stick to you when it's wet."

Despite some dicey moments, my Jeep made it through that day, as far south as I wanted to go, which was a spot just on the edge of the Russell Wildlife Refuge. There's a big prairie dog town there, and a few were popping up from holes. Just around a bend in the road stands a decaying old cabin that was once a homesteader's attempt to stick to the land, the frame now falling down and forlorn. Its falling is what allows the prairie dogs to return. Ranchers poison them; federal money has done so for one hundred years and still does sponsor a war on the little rodents, so a dog town of this scale, maybe four or five hundred acres, is a rare thing. Yet old-timers from this very place say they used to make the day-long ride from the Breaks to Zortman, about sixty miles and, for the entire stretch, rode in one continuous prairie dog town.

The ranchers say they eradicate for the sake of economy and that those of us who would bring the rodents back are impractical preservationists and romantics. Depends on what you mean by economy. No matter what you think about the prairie dogs, though, the ranchers and I can agree that this place has a continuous, fundamental economy. It makes grass into protein. It did before whites came. It did before Indians came. This is the way it always was.

I got out of my Jeep and walked to the edge of the dog town, now taking the perspective of a rancher, not a bison. This flat looks for all the world like the rest of the plains, in that it stretches like a tabletop to the horizon, but I know what the bison didn't. I walk a few hundred yards and am, all of a sudden, standing at the edge of a bluff, a steep, bare bank that falls almost vertically for maybe sixty feet to a creek bed below. It is the sort of feature once crucial to economy—a buffalo jump. Archaeologists have confirmed it as one of those places where bands of natives practiced the ancient art of stampede hunting, scaring whole herds off the cliff. It was the method of necessity before horses.

It is impossible to stand here and not conjure the sounds as if they were borne on the winds from then to now. The noise from the cascading mass of breaking bison must have been overwhelming, then the slaughter celebration and feasting below, first hunters, then magpies, wolves, coyotes—scavengers who all made a living off the excess of the plains, delivered to them through methods of the Indians. These methods may seem wasteful, but that assumption would be narrowminded. Nature knows no waste, just alternate paths in the food chain, sun to grass to protein, then back to rot, ashes, and dust.

So given all this, how can anything ranchers do here be called at all harmful? They have not wasted the landscape so much as they have channeled it to an alternative cycle of the food chain, no longer local.

This bison jump lies at the edge of the Wiederrick ranch, a matter of no small pride to Ross and Dan Wiederrick, brothers in their sixties now who spent their whole lives working this ground. The simple frame ranch house is in sight of the buffalo jump. Telegraph Creek—it waters the ranch and provides the little valley that gives the forty-five-thousand-acre holding its anchor—winds along the base of the bison jump. It is a working ranch, not a wasteland by any means. I left the jump one day and watched two enormous bull elk jump the ranch's fences in an easy lope, then canter off to disappear at the horizon line.

Not even a mile down the road from the ranch house stands a rotting, one-room log building not much bigger than a suburbanite's backyard shed. It was the school that Ross and Dan attended, usually just them and two or three other students. They rode horses to school every day, until they were judged old enough to drive in the ranch's Jeep, which was when the elder of the two was seven.

Wiederrick roots run deep in the Breaks, but the brothers were relative newcomers to this particular piece of ground. Ross tells me the longest root traces through their mother's side, who was a Barrett. That strand travels back to a man named Evans, who made his way upriver from Iowa to Fort Benton in the mid-nineteenth century, liked what he saw, and returned to Iowa to learn his wife had died and his children were boarded with a neighbor woman. So he married the neighbor and returned to Montana to ranch, later begetting a daughter who would marry C. E. Barrett, Ross's grandfather. The Barretts ranched along the Missouri River, which is where a young man of the Wiederrick clan of the nearby Larb Hills figured into the picture. He married Ross's mother and went to work for C. E. The whole extended family had been flooded out by the Fort Peck Dam by 1946, which is when they bought the ranch along Telegraph Creek. It became the Wiederrick ranch when C. E. died, then Ross's and Dan's in 1961 when both parents died in a car-train wreck. In 2004, Ross and Dan sold it to the American Prairie Foundation, a conservation group. It was the first transaction in what the group hopes will be more than fifty, acquisitions that will allow it to assemble a 3.5-million-acre public-private prairie preserve centered in the Russell Wildlife Refuge.

≈

I like most ranchers I have met, a claim that can lapse into stereotype. In fact, most I have met do not fall into the Marlboro-man mold that popular culture has made for them. True enough, when in town for celebrations or elected to the state legislature, they posture: prominent and defiant display of Stetson hats, belt buckles, and such. When acting en masse, they tend to turn red-state conservatism to a screaming crimson. But if there is a stereotype that fits, it is that they are individuals, or as Ross Wiederrick put it to me, "Ranchers are people too."

Left to their own devices, they are as likely to adopt an Elmer Fudd ear-floppered hat as a Stetson, three layers of Carhartts and coveralls instead of skin-tight Wranglers. If they have common traits, these are a ready sense of humor and a blunt practicality. Beyond that, they share a trait common to graziers around the world, a class not often considered separate from farmers but that indeed is separate. Globally, graziers have a real affection for and attachment to the animals they herd and, certainly in the case of the Breaks, a real attachment to and affection for the landscape they inhabit.

Given my arguments that cattle grazing has posed the largest threat to the environment of the grassland West, this can sound contradictory, but humanity is complicated. Industrial-strength tourism in national parks, our most revered landscapes, is arguably more damaging than grazing. Our sense of our duty to the landscape, in fact, our self-interest in preserving its integrity, is evolving, and many ranchers are ahead of the rest of us in the process. Recall now that a few of these men and women trace their lineage to homesteaders, people who jumped off trains at Malta and set straightway to plowing up their 360-

acre claims, an activity that created environmental disaster. No one is more aware of this today than the ranchers, some of whom saw it happen. "It's not farm ground. That's why that country hasn't changed in thousands of years," said Ross Wiederrick. Their education, though, goes beyond this awareness. Wiederrick told me the country taught him respect not only for grass but for native grass. "We always felt the native grass was the strongest grass. We tried some imported species, but we never did have much luck with them," he says.

This raises the matter of coevolution, which involves the evolution of species as best adapting to both the conditions of a place and the other species in that place. *Coevolution,* a term invented only in this generation by biologists Paul Ehrlich and Peter Raven, is the linchpin of today's environmentalism. It ought to be our mantra. Those native grasses have fed big grazers in this place for millennia, so they are adapted to both grazing and other conditions of the place. In particular, they maintain their nutritional value into the harsh winter, unlike some exotics. They are the key, then, to wildlife surviving the place's Siberian winters.

Wiederrick's preference for native grasses is no small matter; in fact, it contradicts generations of government policy and "sound science." In the late nineteenth century, the U.S. Department of Agriculture launched a division called the Bureau of Plant Industry, a name that revealed a mindset. The bureau sent botanists—plant explorers, really—to scour the earth, especially Siberia, for plants that might replace the native vegetation of the plains, which science then judged unsuitable. This is why homestead sites throughout the plains still perch within a vegetative moat of Russian olive and Chinese elm.

The major effect of this search on the northern plains, though, was the importation of crested wheatgrass, a Siberian species that quickly greens up in spring and produces spectacularly but carries no nutritional value into winter. Stands of crested wheatgrass are biological deserts. Part of the New Deal work in the area was the widespread, government-subsidized seeding of crested wheatgrass. To this day, one can find local ag agents and ranchers who swear by its virtues and still plant it, but Ross Wiederrick is not among them.

As our understanding of grazing evolves, though, we know its ecology goes further into issues of coevolution. Our native grasses evolved through grazing by bison, not cattle, and while the two are close relatives, they graze in very different ways. Among the differences is a catastrophic boom-bust cycle imposed by bison. That is, a big herd moves into an area, grazes it to the nubs and otherwise roughs up the landscape, then leaves, sometimes for years. The grasses and other plants have evolved not only to adapt to but to thrive on the booms and busts. That is, the plants fare worse in the absence of these cycles than in their presence, and they suffer under the persistent and steady munching of penned cattle.

This realization led to the practice of what is called rotational grazing, meaning ranchers fence off individual pastures, then move cattle from pasture to pasture, as the bison would have moved about the open range. The Wiederrick brothers were pioneers in rotational grazing. Gus Hormay, an early, nationally known advocate of rotational grazing, came to the Wiederrick ranch in 1970, and the brothers adopted the system shortly thereafter. Wiederrick says the better results were immediate. By attempting to mimic nature, the ranch became more profitable. This management practice, coupled with some improved cattle genetics, has resulted in a spring calf now weighing about six hundred pounds at market time in the fall, compared with less than half of that a generation ago. "Anytime you can raise a six-hundred-pound calf in that hard-pan, greasewood, cactus-infested country, you must be doing something right," said Ross Wiederrick.

This, coupled with their obvious affection for the place, makes it difficult to understand why the Wiederricks would agree to sell the ranch to anyone, let alone a conservation group. Ross Wiederrick said, in contrast to what his neighbors reported, that the cattle business was good for him, that there were indeed lean years, but that overall his ranch was profitable in recent years. Despite being settled in a nice new house in Malta—his community—he spoke of buying a new ranch, maybe in the Sandhills of Nebraska.

I asked him how he could consider leaving the community where he was born and raised, a place that is home for him in a sense most modern Americans cannot imagine. He pointed to his genial wife, Karen, also born and raised in Montana ranching country. "Home," he said, "is where this woman is."

Karen had been participating throughout the interview, often finishing Ross's sentences, each providing details about the other's history. So I pressed them on why they would sell if times were good and they loved their life. "There comes a time for everything, and sometimes you have to do things you don't want to do," said Ross. Then Karen: "You can kind of see the handwriting on the wall with the [black-footed] ferrets and the prairie dogs."

The nature of the country evolved not just through ranching but also through the social attitudes that have placed wildlife on a higher plane. Wiederrick said he didn't necessarily mind that. He has nothing against the wildlife and probably would have enjoyed the sight of those two bull elk gamboling across his former ranch as much as I did. He said one of the prime benefits of his rotational grazing system was that it made more grass for wildlife as well as his cattle.

But he has sold his ranch to a conservation group. Doesn't it rankle this lifelong cattleman that the land he so valued will now be dedicated solely to wildlife? "That's really up to the people that buy it how they run it. I guess I don't really have too big a problem with it," he said.

❧

The fall of that same year, I hiked a coulee on what was the Wiederrick ranch, four or five miles, on a sunny, warm day. I have spent many days walking the Breaks in fall and have always been shocked at how little is left, as if cows had vacuumed every blade of grass from the landscape. That day, it was as if I had entered a never-never land, miles on miles of waist-high grass waiting to overwinter elk, mule deer, pronghorn, and, in a couple of years, bison on that same stretch of ground. That much grass was there because the cows were gone, plain and simple. But not really so plain and simple. Had the Wiederricks not reasonably managed this landscape, it could not have recovered so quickly, become so luxuriant in only one year. Some of their neighbors' land and most of the BLM land would not recover so quickly.

But there are other matters to account for. I saw only a handful of mule deer that day, despite the gorgeous habitat, no elk, a few lone pronghorn. Hundreds of each should have been there, and perhaps in winter, when times are tough all around, the elk indeed congregate on this bounty. But the ranchers through the years have so pressured state game officials that they have issued more permits to kill big game than they should, so numbers are low now. Given grass and more sensible management, though, they can recover.

There is something to Wiederrick's core argument that the land would be in much worse shape if someone other than ranchers had occupied it for as many years as they have, but this ignores the fact that ranchers were the only ones who could have occupied it for so long. The farmers indeed tried to plow it, and the land evicted them for this sin. That's the biggest reason 80 percent of it remains in native grasses; the land insisted that it be so.

The ranchers then occupied this land as a sort of standoff, and one rigged with federal subsidy at that. There is no question they faced astoundingly harsh conditions and no question that they, too, evolved. They are a sort of coevolved species with this landscape, which has built in them a stubbornness, a determination to stick against all odds. It looks like evolution, but it's not; it has not been encoded in their genes, so the trait is not heritable. The real evolutionary force of the Breaks, the big determining factor that is shaping this landscape now, is that these people's children grow up, go to college, and realize that life need not be so.

"When times get bad and [ranchers] really ought to leave, they might not. Yeah. That's right," said Ross Wiederrick. "But the younger generation is different. They don't come back. It's hard work, and there's really not a lot of return for your work. It's isolated."

᪐

Mike Hedrick, the former manager of the Russell Wildlife Refuge, says a cultural factor makes this country resistant to change. Those who have worked this land regard a wildlife refuge as recreation: looking at birds, hunting, hiking, camping, and other such nonsense. A lifetime of hard work has built into these ranchers an obdurate work ethic. "They think recreation is almost a sin," said Hedrick.

This assessment rings out in Ross Wiederrick's economic justification for what he has done: improving the range, for instance, to raise bigger calves. Wiederrick's insistence on basic economics, in fact, puts us on exactly the right track. We can begin with superficial dollars-and-cents economics. In 2002, the Fish and Wildlife Service completed a study called "Banking on Nature." It could well be taken as a bureaucratic attempt to justify the agency's existence, but I think it goes beyond that. It dovetails nicely with similar studies undertaken independently and on a variety of landscapes across the West. Specifically, the study looked at the economics of recreation on fifteen wildlife refuges. One of them was the Russell.

The Russell Wildlife Refuge is hunted for big game, birds, and fish, every year providing a harvest of protein that nature produces in abundance when left to its own devices. The federal government surveyed hunters and anglers and found that they annually pushed about $11 million into the local economy. Spread that amount over the million acres of the refuge, and it means this partly restored ecosystem pumps about $11 an acre into the local economy, not counting another $1.3 million a year that is added by the thousands of visitors who come just to look at scenery and birds.

Ranchers also spend their money in the local economy. Data from the federal Department of Agriculture for Phillips County indicate that the entire county, which is virtually all agricultural, makes about $10 per acre per year. That's for all the land within the county, including the more productive, irrigated croplands along the Milk River north of the Breaks. The land surrounding the Breaks is the very worst for crops, the most arid. Therefore, that income includes federal subsidy. Without federal subsidy, the land makes about $5 an acre a year. Further, the number used for the subsidy relates only to direct payments and does not account for what ranchers pay for their grazing leases (about 10 percent of the market rate), nor does it account for the mountains of federal money spent buying back the broke homesteads and "improving" that land with corrals, fences, and ponds.

Admittedly this comparison is rough. To begin to assess the picture more precisely, we would need to consider such matters as the BLM's budget (which is largely a subsidy to grazing) in comparison to the Russell Wildlife Refuge's budget (which subsidizes wildlife management), as well as the grazing fees paid to the BLM in comparison to fees paid by hunters for duck stamps, the income that goes to wildlife.

Nonetheless, we have some basis for believing that nature here produces more revenue than agriculture does, given an earlier evaluation of this same idea. It's easy enough to believe that we, the affluent of our postmodern society, can squander money on luxuries such as bird watching and recreational hunting. In fact, when the Department of the Interior was pondering the long-term management of the Russell Wildlife Refuge in the early 1960s, someone ran a series of similar calculations, and, oddly enough, that study found that almost exactly the same ratio obtained: Recreation produced about twice the money per acre as ranching did.

This is the sort of comparison that rankles a lot of people, especially those who suggest "you can't eat the scenery." True enough for people, although cattle can indeed eat the scenery. But the interesting issue here involves the commodity mindset, which holds that the human endeavor and all value in our economy are based on the production of a handful of primary commodities, with food at the center but also oil, minerals, and timber. The commodity producers think the rest of the economy rests on their work, that they are the foundation of the pyramid.

Yet, it is exactly this—the very importance of commodities—that has made them ubiquitous and interchangeable, subject to the whims of global markets. China, Mexico, and India all grow wheat every bit as efficiently as do Montana and North Dakota. Australia, Brazil, and Argentina compete on an equal footing with us for beef money. Those global markets, then, become somewhat capricious, placing farmers at the blunt edge of their harsh realities. That is precisely why we have subsidized them and why their economic lot has been, to put it lightly, uneven. They are in the same business as everyone else. The assumption is, though, they have to be, because that's all the landscape will support.

People don't make a lot of money selling commodities; people make a lot of money selling something unique. The assumption that the western economy is based on wheat, timber, and minerals ignores an enormous part of the West. Remember, California is part of the West, and one of its leading industries, both in terms of revenues and international influence, is filmmaking, the exact antithesis of commodity production. The product is something as ephemeral as story, imagination, illusion. In recent years, the role of the film industry in California has been surpassed by that of the information industry, which produces something as ephemeral as bits and bytes. You can't eat bits and bytes either, but you can make a lot of money on them, not just in California, but also in Utah, Texas, Oregon, Washington, and Idaho, all places that have become hubs for the information industry. They have done so because towns such as Seattle, Portland, and Salt Lake City provide the amenities, especially outdoor recreation, that attract people, especially well-educated and highly paid people. These people become the foundation of the economy. So you can make a living on the scenery after all. Of course, some westerners, even ranchers, have known this for a long time. Recall now the second-generation Coburn of a famous ranch in Phillips County, a man who as early as 1910 gave up ranching to shoot silent movies.

The West and ranchers do have something to sell beyond beef and wheat. We have open space, pristine air, and silence, amenities that will become only more rare as humanity crushes in. We have wildlife, and potentially much more wildlife. And ranchers have their stories, their character, something worth a lot more, both in the immediate sense of dollars and cents and as a cultural resource, than any amount of wheat and beef they might produce. Of course, many of these ranchers would reject this line of logic, and perhaps for good reason. Capitalizing on their lives and place with tourism would necessarily entail contact with the larger society. They are loath to do either, and I don't blame them, not one little bit. I have been in Park City, Sun Valley, and Santa Fe. Tourism is the slipperiest of slopes, the reason I would prefer to consider this matter as Ross Wiederrick might, as one of fundamental economy, of natural capitalism.

The salient fact of prairie economy is that a square yard of soil with a cover of native vegetation contains about twenty square miles of root hairs. This is not a fact easily known; it is much easier to assess vegetation aboveground for the obvious reason, easier to assign graduate students to the business of cutting and weighing stems. Not much is known about what goes on beneath the surface, because few have done the spade work in what biologists call the "rhizosphere." It is this bias that makes us label a wheat field productive and a short-grass prairie less so.

If you cut and weigh the annual above-ground growth of a wheat field and match it against that of a short-grass prairie, the wheat field wins, but not by much. Ignore for a moment that this victory depends on overlooking the subsidy to the wheat field in the form of energy for tractors and such—necessary to cultivate—and the hydrocarbon energy converted from natural gas to fertilizer. Reasonable account-ing wouldn't ignore this, but for the sake of argument we will.

Wheat's victory, however, also depends on ignoring what goes on beneath the ground. Wheat is an annual grass, as are both corn and rice. Those three annual grasses supply something like 70 percent of all human nutrition on the planet. This is no accident but rather the result of a somewhat freakish strategy of annual grasses. They collect solar energy and convert most of it to stem, leaf, and seed (seed be-cause they are annual plants). All biological strategies are accountable to the future, and annuals balance the books by dying each fall but en-suring a next generation. The seed is supplied with an abundant source of carbohydrates to sustain it. We humans and other seed-eaters sim-ply appropriate the carbohydrates.

Perennial plants, for example, prairie plants, have a wholly differ-ent strategy. They account to the future with roots, not seeds. A wheat plant's roots penetrate the soil maybe six to eight inches with a struc-ture the size and form of a full head of human hair when the human is hanging upside down. The prairie plants, in contrast, form a dense, closely packed, and intertwined array of roots that extend downward five to six feet. The fact is, if this biomass is added to what the plants provide aboveground, a prairie, hands-down, is the more productive of the two systems. Of course, like the scenery, the roots are not there for the eating, at least not by humans or grazing animals, so what good are they? They are capital, natural capital.

Those roots are in a very real way an investment, a savings account of solar energy banked against bad years. During the Dust Bowl years, soil scientists repeatedly surveyed the plains and filed grim reports of entire areas with no apparent surviving vegetation. Yet in a few years, most of those areas recovered because of their surviving root systems. The plains have suffered millennia of drought cycles and have devised a strategy appropriate to the place.

The root system is infrastructure, stored productivity that allows future productivity, the very definition of capital goods in economics.

This, though, is not the end of the matter. A second key difference between native and cultivated vegetation is biodiversity. A wheat field holds one species; a prairie, hundreds. The prairie's varied species provide services for one another, the most outstanding being nitrogen fixation, performed by legumes such as lupine, members of the pea family. These unique plants have the ability to pull free nitrogen from the air and fix it in the soil, where it becomes available to its neighbors. Nitrogen is the primary element added by chemical fertilizers. That is to say, the subsidy to a wheat field we disregarded earlier is wholly relevant to our comparative analysis. A prairie supplies its own infrastructure.

This infrastructure spirals to unimaginable complexity when we begin to consider the relationships among the hundreds of plants, not to mention the fauna, among them such key players as microbes, grubs, insects, and nematodes, many of which—in fact, almost all of which—are absent from a wheat field. For instance, consider the despised prairie dog, so assiduously exterminated by the ranchers. Prairie dogs' tunneling brings buried minerals to the surface, where they become available to plants and then to the animals that eat those plants. That's why at least one hundred species of animals show a preference for feeding or living in prairie dog towns.

The greatest expression of all of this productivity is the bison and other massive grazers, such as elk and deer. These in turn link top-end predators, such as wolves, bears, cougars, and humans, to this process. We do not know the full measure of this promise of the prairie, but there are tantalizing indications. We have the accounts of early white explorers on the plains telling of herds of bison stretching to horizon lines, of herds that were in constant motion but still took days to pass a given point. We have modern calculations of the number of bison on the presettlement plains, some based on assumptions about the plains' carrying capacity, some on records of bison killed. All are estimates, but in recent years they have come close to reaching a consensus: a population of about thirty million bison. That is roughly equivalent to the number of cattle now in the same area, a place almost wholly devoted to raising cattle.

But most of cow country does not really raise cattle; it raises calves. Those are then shipped to midwestern feedlots and finished on corn and other grains raised on what used to be the tallgrass prairie of the Mississippi River basin. The tallgrass never supported many bison in presettlement times. Thus, most western beef—namely, those that are finished here—become human protein only with a vast subsidy of corn.

There are further skews in the estimates of capacity. For instance, we have not accounted for elk. Elk may well have been fewer than bison in presettlement times, but by any measure their numbers were enormous. An elk produces almost as much meat as a bison. What forms, then, is an argument that says the great grassland, left to its own devices, was more productive of protein before white settlement and agriculture; that is, all of our enormously subsidized intervention has simply undermined the productivity of the plains.

We can think back now to the spectacular catastrophes of the region, the big die-ups when cattlemen lost about 60 percent of their herds in the 1880s, the plow-ups and the Dust Bowl, and all of these coupled to the steady, inexorable decline of human community, despite an unbroken history of federal subsidy. Most areas of the plains today contain fewer people than they did in presettlement days, which is to say, they supported more people before settlers intervened. We can safely assume that, without subsidy, the plains would be even more depopulated.

Simply, a series of misreadings of this landscape, some well-meaning but misguided, some rooted in greed and obstreperousness, has sapped the landscape's ability to produce. We have spent down the natural capital, which was the soil and the roots, the gentle little streams protected by native vegetation, the wildlife that was supported by all of this and in turn supported it.

This is not, then, an argument about conservation or, more to the point, preservation, not a plan to fence off a small preserve for the privileged to exercise wilderness fantasies. We have transcended that now to begin considering natural capitalism. Stripped to its raw market level, what we demand of the plains today is protein. The promise of the place is that it can indeed deliver that protein, if we learn to respect its limits.

❧

The comparison of the plains to the sea persists throughout European contact with the Great Plains, right on up to today. For instance, the seminal biological study that led to this book is titled *Ocean of Grass.* Yet I am going to extend that analogy one more step here by arguing that we need to begin thinking about the plains the way we think about the fundamental economy of the ocean. Consider, for instance, the salmon, an amazing animal that has fed entire cultures, just as the bison fed plains Indian cultures. And not just Indians have fed on the salmon. Salmon cultures abounded throughout northern Europe and Asia, a circumboreal phenomenon. A vestige of that ancient culture remains today in North America in both Alaska and British Columbia. We understand that, left to its own devices, the ocean will produce an abundant harvest of salmon, and, in fact, we have learned some harsh lessons about those devices and how strict the ocean's limits are. For instance, attempts to farm fish, that is, bring agriculture's methods to the salmon culture, are proving every bit as disastrous as was bringing agriculture to the plains. Also, in regard to native stocks, logging along spawning streams has greatly decreased productivity, so through this we have learned about coevolution, the natural capital of salmon production, and the necessity of a healthy forest as part of that natural capital. Through this increased awareness, we have been able to maintain viable native stocks of salmon in some places, and those animals continue to feed us. A commercial salmon fisherman is a hunter-gatherer.

The biggest challenge in maintaining the wild system is in regulating the take, and the evidence that we have failed to do so is the decline of wild fisheries worldwide. But this is a failure of political will, and in fact we have counterexamples, successes of regulation, such as Maine's lobster industry, local fisheries around Japan, and, to a certain extent, Alaska's salmon fishery. The difference between this system and farming, though, is fundamental. It would not be difficult for a biologist to design fishing regulations that would make wild fisheries sustainable. Forever. It is simply a matter of setting limits and monitoring and reacting to changes in weather, cycles, and currents, cutting back in lean times, and understanding what is surplus and what is natural capital but never spending down the capital.

In contrast, the biologist Stuart L. Pimm said—and he's right—that no biologist, or anyone else for that matter, could design a system of regulations that would make agriculture sustainable. Sustainable agriculture is an oxymoron. It mostly relies on an unnatural system of annual grasses grown in a monoculture, a system that nature does not sustain or even recognize as a natural system. We sustain it with plows, petrochemicals, fences, and subsidies, because there is no other way to sustain it.

Of course there was a short period of neo-European history when we did treat the plains exactly as we treated the ocean, a period of market hunting. The result was the near extermination of the bison, antelope, elk, ducks, and geese and the complete extermination of the passenger pigeon, shot by the millions with punt guns and packed in barrels for eastern tables. Out of that experience, as we have seen, evolved a system of sport hunting, at first an elitist pastime, formalized as Theodore Roosevelt's Boone and Crockett Club, which was then and is now primarily an organization that measures antlers. It legitimizes the "mine's bigger than yours" game, fundamental to male behavior. Trophy hunting has not much to do with sustainability, either.

But in the process, we learned to regulate and we built, not just in the elite, but in most hunters, an ethic that places conservation of the species foremost. As with trophy hunting, however, that ethic won't get us where we need to go. The governing mythology of hunting is still about trophies, about the big and the bold, so it stands the rules of predation on their head. That's not to say this mythology has to go away. A restored plains wilderness would indeed have room for sport hunting, for that legitimate need that some of us have not just for wild protein but for venturing into a wild landscape, observing, breathing the wildness of a place—for experience as well as protein. This is the sort of activity that enriches lives as it enriches landscapes.

Beyond that, for the plains to return to what they once were, we as a society will need to learn to conduct regulated market hunting, to behave as predators. Recall now that overheard conversation of Montana ranchers, who spent most of their time figuring out how to keep wildlife from taking over their land so they could raise cattle—that is, how to remove elk and deer, big hunks of protein, so that they could raise protein. The plains, despite their abuse, are never really very far from the wild. Wildlife wants to happen there.

So what would happen if you gave those ranchers the right to sell that wild protein, first by charging sport hunters, but second by market hunting to cull the does and smaller deer the sport hunters don't take? What if wildlife became more lucrative than cows? What if ranchers had every financial incentive to restore habitat, remove cows, and live among wildlife?

Economy can indeed have an enormous role in resurrecting the plains. The nineteenth century made market hunting taboo, or at least market hunting on land. Commercial fishing is tolerated, even revered, and it is market hunting. It is time to raise a serious discussion that would erase this taboo.

Eleven

A BEGINNING

In October 2005, sixteen bison stepped off a trailer and onto the former Wiederrick ranch in the Missouri Breaks, there to stay, a milestone in the progress of the American Prairie Foundation. It was no small feat but rather the result of years of research, itself a measure of the project's attentiveness to the wild. There may be three hundred thousand animals called bison today, but those that are the real deal are a good bit more scarce.

All of those remaining have descended from the bottleneck population of a handful of animals at the turn of the twentieth century. The iconic herds are those in such places as Yellowstone National Park, Wind Cave National Park, in South Dakota, and the Theodore Roosevelt National Park, in North Dakota, but these are not the bulk of the population. The vast majority of bison are in private herds spread throughout the West, largely on commercial ranches raising bison for slaughter. Many of those animals challenge the definition of bison. The conditions of the private herds range widely from animals handled and raised more or less as wild animals to those that live not much differently from feedlot cattle, penned and force-fed corn. The more serious issue, however, goes to the very genetic core.

As soon as bison became available for private ranching in the late

nineteenth century, those who owned them almost immediately began tinkering by cross-breeding them to cattle, an act that is doable
but with some difficulty. The nadir of this sort of activity was marked
with an active marketing campaign of something branded (in the modern use of the word) as a "beefalo." The result of all of this is that most
of those three hundred thousand animals remaining, including some
of the more highly touted wild herds, have some cattle genes.

I began this discussion by noting that the project in the Missouri
Breaks was based on some sound biology, specifically, the inventory
of remaining grassland systems in the northern plains, presented in
Ocean of Grass. It was a landmark in conservation in that it asked the
question of possibility: Where is the best remaining habitat? Where
might we have the best possibilities for success in conservation? This
is the study that identified ten such sites in the northern plains and
singled out the Missouri Breaks as the best of those. This same study
proposed staking out a 3.5-million-acre reserve in the Breaks, a size
predicated on the requisite amount of habitat for a sufficient population of bison to support wolves, again wise biology. Working ecosystems are not simply an à la carte assembly of animals we would like to
see. Such ecosystems are not complete until they contain the most
threatened, and the most threatened worldwide are the top-end predators, wolves in the case of the Great Plains.

Reintroduction of the bison into the Breaks was guided by some
equally sound science. World Wildlife Fund biologists Curtis Freese
and Steve Forrest, two of the same people who wrote *Ocean of Grass,*
commissioned researchers at Texas A&M University to use DNA
markers to seek out genetically pure herds of bison. They found three
such herds in the United States, including two of the icons but also,
oddly enough, one private herd belonging to Ted Turner, located on
one of his ranches in New Mexico. The sixteen animals reintroduced
into the Missouri Breaks, however, came from a public herd, the one
at Wind Cave National Park. In the spring of 2006, the young cows

among those now in the Breaks dropped five calves, and so it begins. Of course, the reintroduction drew the full media treatment, with major stories playing around the world. The stories were an easy sell, so central is this animal to the American imagination.

Thus, we mark a bit of progress in the work of the American Prairie Foundation, the local nonprofit fostered by the World Wildlife Fund to carry out this important bit of work. Other marks of progress have occurred as well. The group has raised millions of dollars to go about its main business: acquiring land. The Wiederrick ranch was the first, but as of late 2008 the organization has gained control of 71,000 more acres, either deeded or leased. Thus, in the long tradition of conservation the foundation labors to assemble a dream involving 3.5 million acres, a process projected to take twenty years and to cost at least three hundred million dollars, about as much money as the United States spends in less than two days on the Iraq war. The bison are back, the land base is growing, and the money is coming in, so if all of this activity continues apace for two decades, the foundation will be able to draw that big circle, look to the bison, wolves, prairie dogs, ferrets, and such within, and say that once again American conservation has been able to do what American conservation does best; it will have established a viable wildlife preserve, one that is unique in the nation's portfolio of preserves.

Yet consider this against what you now know of the history of this place as it winds through the very center of America's relationship with itself and nature. To an astounding degree, the central contradictions of American conservation play out in rich detail on this very landscape. Will we do justice to this history and this place if we simply create one more preserve where tourists might gawk, videotape, and spend money? Not by my reckoning. The *Ocean of Grass* study teased out an opportunity that it did not explicitly recognize, but I do. This place, this very spot, is the best opportunity we have not just to restore a landscape but to move the very idea of conservation beyond the industrialist mindset that has shaped it. So far, conservation has been defined by removing nature from economy. What I demand of this place is that we reconcile nature and economy to create a working landscape, one that works but also does work.

Arid landscapes favor pastoralists over farmers; they are the lands of Abel, not Cain. In Montana, grasslands beget ranchers; in Kenya, they favor people like the Masai, in the southern part of the country, and their close relatives, the Samburus, who have for thousands of years herded sheep, goats, and cattle in the sweeping grasslands around Mount Kenya, in the north. Today the population of about 150,000 Samburus is plagued by violence and poverty; their lands are overgrazed.

Telling a Samburu herder he is overgrazing is telling him he has too many cattle, which is saying he is too rich. Telling him to protect wildlife is telling him to harbor the enemy; elephants do indeed seek out cattle and stomp them to death, so Samburu warriors kill elephants with their four-foot-long spears. Probably also best not to ask a Samburu's opinion of the rich British ranchers who fenced off huge areas of Samburu territory to deprive them of their millennia-old habit of nomadism. Unless, of course, that rancher is Ian Craig, a third-generation Kenyan, who took over his parents' 62,000-acre ranch in 1977. He was a hunting guide then and not at all interested in raising cattle, so he sold his and eventually stocked the place with wildlife, especially the endangered black rhinoceros.

Nothing is inherently wrong with grazing. As we've seen, grasses and shrubs, in fact, coevolved with big grazers and browsers to the point that the flora actually prospers when grazed by the proper animals at the proper time. Craig used wildlife—by definition, the species that coevolved with the place—to restore the landscape. One enters the ranch, now called the Lewa Conservancy, from the drought-dried, cow-burned Samburu lands around it, and it looks green and lush, feeling five degrees cooler. The ranch holds 425 Grevy's zebras, or 20 percent of Kenya's total population of that endangered species, and 37 black rhinos, or 8 percent of Kenya's total.

Craig's wildlife, however, harmed neighboring Samburu communal ranches when the animals migrated between the conservancy and the Samburu National Reserve to the north. The Samburu retaliated by killing some of the conservancy's elephants. Craig's solution to this conflict was money. He convinced the leaders of a neighboring Samburu communal ranch to create wildlife areas on their own land by reducing numbers of livestock. He used money donated by NGOs, philanthropists, and American zoos to create an umbrella organization, the Northern Rangelands Trust, which is a squad of experts who teach interested Samburus everything from rotational grazing and wildlife management to microlending and guest lodge strategy. Eight Samburu communal ranches have signed on now, creating a mosaic of 1.5 million acres of wildlife habitat between Craig's 62,000-acre ranch and the 74,000-acre complex of game reserves anchored by the Samburu National Reserve. Each Samburu community has built or is building an upscale guest lodge. Wildlife is building the economy, which in turn is building and staffing clinics and schools.

Given that the world has many farmers and lots of corn, do inhabitants of arid lands help themselves best by trying to grow a few more kilos of corn or by offering for sale the precious experience of watching black rhinos, Grevy's zebras, lions, and Samburu herders in a single survey of a broad, grassy plain? Good economics favor wildlife in Kenya, but I suspect they can also teach us something about the American plains.

⁊

The story goes that when rich white men first began to take sporting forays into the northern Great Plains, they brought with them the unwieldy canvas wall tents long used successfully east of the Mississippi. The natives thought these were terribly ungainly structures and laughed openly at them. They, of course, preferred the tipi, exotic to white eyes, but a structure time tested and coevolved with prairie conditions. It is said the natives found even more mirth in wall tents when the first good blow came on and tore them all to shreds. Tipis may look odd, but their conical shape withstands a prairie's fierce winds; they are of an evolutionary design, tested just as natural selection tests and shapes a species of animal. Conservation is about respect for natural selection's evolved solutions to inhabiting a place.

I was on one of the first "safaris" for the American Prairie Foundation in 2002 and have been on maybe a half dozen since, and, yes, the foundation insisted on naming these forays exactly that, despite imagery of rich white men descending on the colonies for a bit of sport. The trips were indeed gatherings of rich people, maybe six or eight at a time, plus those of us on hand to explain the natural and human history of the landscape. They were, for these people, undoubtedly enriching events. Most of them had never seen this landscape and the wildlife inhabiting it. Some were daunted. I remember one case in which a newcomer had to go sit in a car for a while after being rendered disoriented and dizzy by the lack of vertical referents.

The object of these trips was to impress these people sufficiently so that they would write checks for the work ahead, and this approach is no anomaly. It is, in fact, how most conservation is done in the United States, over wine and cheese and PowerPoint presentations, a process that reliably produces checks.

And, yes, these rich people, at least in the beginning, slept in wall tents. And, yes indeed, they did blow down in one fierce storm I remember. But as the organization matured, it meant to provide more permanent habitation for its safaris, and some of us associated with the project, especially those of us who knew the tipi story, as I did, suggested to the foundation's director, Sean Gerrity, that these more permanent structures should be tipis. Gerrity vetoed that, telling me rather directly that he could not ask rich people to sleep in tipis. Instead, he ordered up a batch of yurts, evolved structures of the Mon-

golian steppe, and erected them on some wood platforms. Came the
first stiff windstorm, and the yurts blew down.

The problem with the way we raise money for conservation in this
country is that it skews the agenda toward the wishes of the donors.
Donors may not know much about the subject at hand but nonetheless are not the least bit hesitant, to varying degrees, about making some
stiff demands as to how their money is spent. This may be understandable, but it colors the judgment of some who disburse the money,
especially so in this case.

In 2001, Gerrity was recruited by the World Wildlife Fund biologist Curtis Freese, a friend of his in Bozeman, Montana, to run the
project. Gerrity had recently moved to Bozeman after selling his business consulting firm in California's Silicon Valley. He had no experience doing conservation. Further, he first recruited donors and board
members from among his contacts in Silicon Valley, a culture renowned
for its arrogance and penchant for control. This was before the dot-
com bust of 2001, so arrogance was at a particularly robust level. I have
not only participated on safaris but also attended meetings of the group
and could not help but sense a whiff of the wood-paneled New York
study where Teddy Roosevelt and Andrew Carnegie began bison conservation. It was a rich man's sport then and remains so now, and much
good can come from simply raising money. At the time, the American Prairie Foundation's job was to buy land as rapidly as possible, and
that is done with money. In charge of this, I likely would have done
much the same. Furthermore, I do not question the donors' motives.
All I've met have been well-meaning; a few are dedicated and skilled
conservationists—not enough, but a few. Nonetheless, the nature of
the arrangement can go down hard, especially on such occasions as
hearing one donor summarize a safari by telling Gerrity, "Without
you, we'd just be another bunch of rich people with nothing to do."

The culture skewed the agenda, and Gerrity made some critical errors in the early going. First, he stacked the board with donors, most

of them not from Montana, and this exclusion was not just at the board level. He also consciously dissociated from conservationists. Montana is a fortunate place in that it has an active and committed community of career conservationists, most of whom have taken some very hard knocks through the years and learned their business the hard way. And learn they did, to the point that the community is not riven with the internecine warfare that separates conservationists elsewhere. They win by specializing in various skills and working together to complement one another.

For instance, in the 2004 state legislative elections, this community launched an initiative to ban the mining of gold by heap leaching it with cyanide, a noxious tactic that has degraded several streams in the state. This way of mining gold is still the most economic, so passing this ban was tantamount to banning new gold mines in a state founded on mining. Come the election, this blatant environmental initiative passed the voters' muster by two-thirds. During the same election, George W. Bush carried the state by 20 percent.

Gerrity's snubbing of this community raised a lot of hackles, particularly among those who had joined the *Ocean of Grass* study, which identified the American Prairie Foundation's project. His decision was particularly galling in the case of keeping the National Wildlife Federation at arm's length, a personal snub. The federation's longtime point man in Montana is Tom France, who has spent nearly thirty years fighting conservation's legal battles. He was the lawyer who won the case that gave control of the Charles M. Russell National Wildlife Refuge to the Fish and Wildlife Service, the legal battle that put the refuge on the road to real conservation so that it might today provide the core of the foundation's project.

Beyond this, Gerrity adopted a sort of culture of deception that might be perfectly understandable in Silicon Valley's competitive confines but builds distrust when one is dealing with the public and public lands. For instance, for several years, he refused to disclose in public discussions the fact that the foundation had targeted 3.5 million acres, despite broadly sharing that number with donors, along with specific maps.

All of this built an atmosphere, even a deserved reputation for the project, of elitism and arrogance. My guess is, the missteps have set the project back several years. Nonetheless, this is an almost normal course of events in the evolution of a conservation movement. It is said in biology that ontogeny recapitulates phylogeny, meaning the developmental stages of an individual embryo look like the evolutionary developmental stages of its species. The evolution of the American Prairie Foundation began with the ethic of the nineteenth century. As I write this, though, signs of change are occurring, and I have no doubt that the soundness of the concept and the considerable evolutionary forces of Montana politics will press the organization to correct these missteps. If we have learned anything from the history of this particular place, it is that its inhabitants have an almost teleological ability to reject unsound ideas and bad behavior. This is a big project requiring a long view, which quickly moves us away from these organizational difficulties. The long view suggests my criticisms above are nitpicking, but even if these minor mistakes had not been made, even if the foundation had flawlessly gone about the business of raising money and buying land, this project would be way too narrow in its goals and would fail the mandate that history and biology have provided. I hope the project becomes far more than just another rich man's plot with a fence around it. It must reconnect conservation to economy. What might this look like?

The knee-jerk reaction to the economics of conservation leads straightway to tourism. Indeed, we already have before us the studies that say the Russell Wildlife Refuge makes more per acre on tourism and hunting at this point than does the surrounding agricultural land. No doubt, the tourism aspect will continue to grow, but from the conservationist's point of view, this is a slippery slope. Tourism does have an upside besides generating income. Seeing the landscape and the creatures that inhabit it does go a long way toward building the appreciation and political support nature needs. But we have only to consider the problems of the nation's parks to see some of the downsides. The two oldest parks, Yellowstone and Yosemite, are jammed and thoroughly commercialized, especially the latter. Industrial-strength tourism can be every bit as damaging to the environment as agriculture. This is not the best link or even a solid one between nature and economy.

A better link, as I have argued above, is protein, and indeed the Prairie Foundation does plan to keep all of its land open to hunters, under proper restrictions. The resulting hunting will generate income, but, more important, it is fundamentally productive. Montana hunters—this one included—tend to completely replace commercial beef and pork in their diets with what they shoot. Every elk I shoot is one fewer cow through a feedlot, one fewer cornfield cut to fatten it, countless doses of antibiotics saved. Yet sport hunting has its problems. Hunters concentrate on large males among wildlife, while the natural selection of predators hits different age classes and both sexes. So should the Prairie Foundation consider experiments with commercial slaughter to complement hunting? Probably, but it's way too soon to tell. We have not seen in detail a working prairie landscape in more than a century. We have never seen a restored prairie landscape work. Much of this will depend on the dynamic that establishes among the ungulates and predators.

Still, we need to prepare for some massive and controlled kills. Though the planned preserve is enormous, it is still not big enough. Drought can and will strike every inch of it at some point, especially as the northern plains slip into global warming. Managers will need to reduce populations drastically to weather those cycles, simply because the big grazers can't migrate hundreds of miles to escape drought, as they did on the presettlement plains.

Seeing the preserve as simply a hunting opportunity, however, may well underestimate its possibilities. I can imagine the landscape evolving as a series of concentric circles, the innermost being the prairie preserve. Restored to its productivity, it will produce wildlife in great abundance. But some of the wildlife, and certainly some of what we learn about maintaining the productivity of this restored landscape, will spill beyond the preserve's borders onto private land. This will raise all sorts of opportunities for commercial hunting and commercial bison herds, which in turn will likely also support the local processing of meat and hide tanning, as well as tourism and dude ranching.

But even this scenario involves thinking way too narrowly about the land in terms of market commodities. One of the reasons America's rural landscape is so badly abused is that the market undervalues the landscape, its ability to produce real and economically valuable amenities beyond beef and wheat. The most promising and rapidly emerging market at this writing is carbon sequestration; that is, utilities that generate power from hydrocarbons, but also many other industries that generate carbon dioxide, are beginning to pay for reforestation projects so that forests simply exist. Forests are carbon sinks, in that they pull carbon dioxide from the air and lock it up in biomass. But prairies do this too, storing the carbon in that deep network of roots, all of which is biomass. This is not theoretical; in fact, in Montana, experiments have been done that assign real and demonstrable values to the grasslands' abilities to store carbon. As those carbon sequestration markets develop, and they will, especially if the United States finally signs on to international agreements to reduce carbon emissions, a restored prairie landscape is a salable carbon sink.

Think also about the thousands of ponds that dot the landscape, damming every stream and seep and making a dewatered system. Much of that pond water simply evaporates during the scorching summers of the Breaks. Restoration of this landscape necessitates that these dams be breached and the protective cover of streamside riparian vegetation be restored. Under these conditions, far less water will evaporate, sedimentation will be greatly reduced, and more and cleaner water will flow to the Missouri River. People, mostly shippers downstream, fight long and hard over Missouri River water. So why not sell the runoff of the prairie to downstream shippers and irrigators? It's already a common practice elsewhere.

These are but a couple of possibilities, but they head us away from the creation of just another rich man's plot of land with a fence around it and toward the creation of a working landscape. The value of this land restoration can extend far beyond this prairie. It can show us some of the ways that nature maintains us and can teach our markets to value the landscape for all it does.

If the history of the Breaks teaches us nothing else, it is that American conservation coevolved with changing attitudes toward public lands. We had no concept of public lands in the beginning, but starting with the parks and forest preserves, we slowly came to the conclusion that not all land should be diced up and sold. We do in fact have, especially in the West, a commons. Abuses of that commons by graziers and loggers notwithstanding, public lands are among our nation's proudest achievements. Beyond providing a commons, they allow us to think in terms of layers of values. Land is many things to many people, not simply a factory for single commodities.

The American Prairie Foundation has so far said it will hold the lands it acquires and will work with the federal and state governments to manage the whole. This does not go far enough. It has said it will leave the lands open to public access, as it must, but this, too, does not go far enough. The people behind this project will eventually smack up against the native distrust of outsiders owning land, both among the local ranchers and more broadly, across the state, among liberal and conservative alike. To win public trust, the foundation must do what has often been done in these cases and give the land back to the federal government, specifically the Fish and Wildlife Service. These must become public lands, managed as a commons. The history of this place demands it.

But there is an odd thing about this landscape: It seems to get what it demands. This is the basis of my fascination with grassland landscapes; they slowly, inexorably, return to what they wish to be. Despite my reservations with some of the initial actions of the Prairie Foundation, I still have little doubt that this project will succeed, largely as imagined, because it was actually not imagined but rather read from the changing face of the land. The biologists who conducted the *Ocean of Grass* study and triggered this work were being not prescriptive but descriptive. This preserve has been coming, evolving in all its facets, for more than a century. Throughout that history, countless human errors have occurred on this landscape, but the land has corrected them, has continued, with some help here and there, toward what it wishes to be.

A few more mistakes will not change this. Eventually the Breaks will break us, teach us to live within their rules.

ACKNOWLEDGMENTS

This book, like any, arises from the thoughts, the writings, and the conversation of others. My job as a journalist is to collect and deliver these to you, so my primary debt here is to the people behind these thoughts, publications, and conversations. I have followed the journalistic habit of acknowledging them as they appear in the text or in the notes below, but honesty requires that I restate the debt here.

Beyond this, any writer who climbs onto a soapbox has a rare stroke of luck when someone has already taken the time to construct a sturdy and appropriate platform to support the weight of his arguments. That was the case here, to a far greater degree than any writer has reason to expect. I have acknowledged this in the text, but it bears repeating here. The framework both for the American Prairie Foundation's project and for this work was wonderfully laid out in the study titled *Ocean of Grass.*

Those of us who think and write about nature today are far more fortunate than our predecessors, in that we have a mature science to guide us. The sophisticated mapping and analysis that drove *Ocean of Grass* is a highly developed example. Specifically, a coalition of conservation groups deserves great credit for that work, for driving their advocacy with state-of-the-art reasoning, and, finally, for acting as a coalition. We are all indebted to the Sierra Club, the World Wildlife Fund, the Conservation Alliance of the Great Plains, Defenders of Wildlife, Central Montana Wildlands Association, Prairie Hills Audubon Society of Western South Dakota, Alberta Wilderness Association, Biodiversity Conservation Alliance, Grasslands Naturalists, Wildlands Project, the Denver Zoo, Badlands Conservation Alliance, the Big Open, the Center for Native Ecosystems, Big Sky Conservation Institute, and Predator Conservation Alliance for this seminal piece of work. We are also indebted to the Nature Conservancy for earlier and complementary analyses.

The second prop of this book was financial. My friend Susan O'Connor, whose family, among other endeavors, provides immeasurable support to conservation throughout the world through the Charles Engelhard Foundation, saw fit to back my work for two years. Serious journalism is no longer commercially viable in our society, so independent writers need financial support. Susan is wise enough to recognize this and to provide that support with no strings attached. Additionally, Susan has joined the American Prairie Foundation's board and works tirelessly for that project. She and her husband, Roy O'Connor, put their labors, hearts, and minds as well as their money into the cause of conservation, and we all owe them a lot because of it. I thank them not only for their support but also for their friendship.

This work is also indebted to the American Prairie Foundation itself, as well as to individuals on its board and staff. Sean Gerrity, Curt Freese, and Steve Forrest were particularly helpful in granting interviews, time, and access to information and in tolerating the aggravations raised by the demands of a writer's work. The foundation gave me full access to its information, to many of its internal deliberations, and especially to the landscape itself. My friend Sarah Davies, formerly of the foundation's staff, was a blessing throughout. The affable Harry Wilson, a board member, prodded in some proper places.

Likewise, I was aided in gathering information by the staffs at Montana State University's Special Collections Library, the Montana

Historical Society Archive at Helena, and the Mansfield Library at the University of Montana.

Some of the thinking in this book was condensed to a magazine article that appeared in *OnEarth* magazine, and I thank George Black, my editor on that project, for helping to shape my thinking.

Of course, any book is nothing without publication, so I am indebted to Jenny Wapner, the project's sponsoring editor, for believing in the book enough to want to print it, to Matthew Winfield, along with several reviewers, for helpful comments and corrections, and to University of California Press's editorial board for seeing it through.

Finally, as I have done for seven books, I acknowledge for this one and for all future work that none of it would exist without my wife, Tracy Stone-Manning, a true and incomparable partner in a writer's life. Her own work for conservation has become—literally—a force of nature. She is an inspiration both for me and for a similarly undeserving world.

NOTES

1. VISION

1. Catlin 1973: 258.
2. Catlin 1973: 258.
3. Licht 1977: 20.
4. Manning 2004: 52, derived from statistics of the Food and Agriculture Organization of the United Nations.
5. Henwood 1998.
6. Forrest et al. 2004.

2. ABORIGINAL SINS

1. Porter 2002: 12.
2. Manning 1995: 28 (from a Bureau of Land Management report).
3. White 1991: 119.
4. Webb 1931: 143.
5. Isenberg 2000: 58.
6. Isenberg 2000: 35; Malone et al. 1991: 20–21.
7. Catlin 1973: letter four.
8. Isenberg 2000: 91.
9. Evans 1998: 46–53.
10. Crosby 1986: 182–87.
11. Isenberg 2000: 26.

12. Porter 2002: 11–12.
13. Flores 2001: 62–64.
14. Isenberg 2000: 92.
15. Catlin 1973: 253.
16. Catlin 1973: 47.
17. Grinell, letter of transmittal, quoted from Dana 1876: 61.
18. White 1991: 338.
19. White 1991: 338.
20. Isenberg 2000: 144.
21. Isenberg 2000: 147.
22. Isenberg 2000: 152.
23. Isenberg 2000: 155.
24. Connell 1984: 362.
25. Whitman, quoted in Connell 1984: 363.
26. Manning 1995: 88.
27. Morris 1979: 224.
28. Morris 1979: 224.

3. PROPERTY WAS THEFT

Epigraphs: Howard 1943: 22; Toole 1959: 44.

1. Silliman 1974.
2. Milner 1987.
3. Morris 1979: 278.
4. White 1991: 333.
5. Armington 1959: 7–8.
6. Quoted in Howard 1943: 120.
7. Stuart 1977: 151.
8. Stuart 1977: 157.
9. Malone et al. 1991: 157.
10. Miller 1940: 8.
11. Stuart 1977: 236–37.
12. Stuart 1977: 188.
13. Quoted in Webb 1931: 288.
14. Peffer 1951: 79.
15. Howard 1943: 32.
16. Peffer 1951: 22–23.
17. Miller 1940: 65.

4. FACE IT TO LIVE

1. *Phillips County News*, quoted in Miller 1940: 33–36.
2. *Phillips County News*, quoted in Miller 1940: 36.
3. Interview with Randy Matchett, 2004, at his Ferret Camp in the Missouri Breaks, personal collection.

5. ALL HELL NEEDS

Epigraph: quoted in Foss 1960: 20.

1. Powell, quoted in Webb 1931: 2.
2. Peffer 1951: 9.
3. Quoted in Peffer 1951: 144.
4. Morris 1979: 382–83.
5. Isenberg 2000: 169.
6. Miller 1940: 52–53.
7. Miller 1940: 53.
8. Morris 2001: 231.
9. Morris 2001: 221.
10. Peffer 1951: 102.
11. Morris 2001: 516.
12. Hill, quoted in Martin 1976: 550.

6. NOTHING CAME UP THAT YEAR

Epigraph: Hill, quoted in Malone et al. 1991: 241.

1. White 1991: 196.
2. Martin 1976: 69.
3. Hill, quoted in Martin 1976: 294.
4. Martin 1976: 301.
5. Quoted in Miller 1940: 55.
6. Quoted in Miller 1940: 48.
7. Montana Land Use Planning Section 1938: 8.
8. Montana Land Use Planning Section 1938: 29.
9. Montana Land Use Planning Section 1938: 29.
10. Malone et al. 1991: 240.
11. Malone et al. 1991: 232–53.
12. Howard 1943: 189.
13. Malone et al. 1991: 243.
14. White 1991: 433.

15. Howard 1943: 192.
16. Malone et al. 1991: 280–88.
17. Miller 1940: 69.

7. PAVING THE ROAD TO HELL

Epigraphs: Powell, quoted in Lowitt 1984: 62; Wallace, quoted in Montana Land Use Planning Section 1938: 60–61.

1. McDonald 2002: 152–76.
2. Howard 1943: 303–4.
3. Elmer Starch, interviewed in Wilson 1951–56.
4. Information to Go to Farmers on Land Plans (1934). Oddly, those deeds had surfaced only a few days before I saw them; a local title company had stored them in Malta ever since the Depression and had finally cleared them out, sending them off to the local county museum to see whether anyone there could make use of them.
5. Wilson 1951–56: 50.
6. Wilson 1951–56: 53.
7. Dean 1984: 52.
8. Wilson 1951–56: 318–19.
9. Wilson 1951–56: 873.
10. Wilson 1951–56: 871.
11. Hickock, quoted in Beasley 1982: 58–62.
12. Lantz 1935.
13. Starch, quoted in Wilson 1951–56: 1522–23.
14. Starch, quoted in Wilson 1951–56: 1507–9.
15. Wooten 1965: 18.
16. Edward Taylor, quoted in Peffer 1951: 217.
17. Foss 1960: 82; Schlebecker 1963: 161.
18. Rivenes 1988.

8. THE UNWILD WEST

Epigraphs: Schlebecker 1963: 1941; Svobida, quoted in Murphy 2003: 64.

1. Freidel 1990: 276.
2. Stockmen Approve New Grazing Area within Three County Limits (1934).
3. Peffer 1951: 332.

4. Carpenter, quoted in Foss 1960: 119.
5. Foss 1960: 86.
6. Peffer 1951: 276.
7. Foss 1960: 136.
8. Pearlstein 2005.
9. Wuerthner 2002: 247–48.
10. Cited in Wuerthner 2002: 247–50.
11. Wuerthner 2002: 247–50.
12. Tape-recorded interview by Charles Barnard, personal collection, Malta, MT.

9. CONSERVATION'S CONTRADICTION

Epigraph: Peffer 1951: 331.
1. Brant 1988: 4.
2. Watkins 1990: 457.
3. Brant 1988: 4.
4. Coleman, quoted in Saindon 1977: 35.
5. One Hundred Fifty Live in Tent Town (1934).
6. Saindon 1977: 39.
7. Watkins 1990: 384.
8. Watkins 1990: 378.
9. Watkins 1990: 464.
10. Watkins 1990: 469.
11. Executive Order no. 7509, December 11, 1936.
12. U.S. Fish and Wildlife Service 1984: 1.
13. U.S. Fish and Wildlife Service 1963.
14. U.S. Fish and Wildlife Service 1984: 2.
15. Tape-recorded interview with Mike Hedrick, Lewiston, MT, March 9, 2004, personal collection. All of Hedrick's quotations in this volume are taken from this interview.

10. A LEARNED LEGACY

Epigraph: Tape-recorded interview with Ross Wiederrick, Malta, MT, March 10, 2004, personal collection. All of Wiederrick's quotations in this chapter are taken from this interview.

BIBLIOGRAPHY

Argument Arises over Statement of Commissioner: Dr. Elwood Mead Stirs Up Controversy by Asserting Eastern Montana and Western North Dakota Must Be Turned to Grazing. 1934. *Saco Independent*, August 2, 1A, Saco, MT.

Armington, Bill. 1959. Interview typescript. Montana Historical Society Archives, Helena.

Beasley, M. H. 1982. Lorena Hickock to Harry Hopkins, 1933: A Woman Reporter Views Hard Times on the Prairie. *Montana: The Magazine of Western History* 32: 58–67.

Boyd, D. P. 2003. Conservation of North American Bison: Status and Recommendations. Master's thesis, Faculty of Environmental Design, Calgary, University of Calgary.

Brant, I. 1988. *Adventures in Conservation with Franklin D. Roosevelt.* Flagstaff, AZ: Northland Publishing Company.

Catlin, G. 1973. *Letters and Notes on the Manners, Customs, and Conditions of North American Indians.* New York: Dover Publications.

Colleran, Tom. 1988. Interview, tape recording. Montana Historical Society Archives, Helena.

Connell, E. S. 1984. *Son of the Morning Star.* San Francisco: North Point Press.

Crosby, A. W. 1986. *Ecological Imperialism.* Cambridge: Cambridge University Press.

Culver, J. C., and J. Hyde. 2000. *American Dreamer: The Life and Times of Henry A. Wallace.* New York: W. W. Norton.

Daily, G. C. 2002. *The New Economy of Nature: The Quest to Make Conservation Profitable.* Washington DC: Island Press.

Dana, G. B. 1876. *Geological Report: Reconnaissance from Carroll, Montana to Yellowstone National Park.* Washington DC, War Department.

Evans, L. T. 1998. *Feeding the Ten Billion: Plants and Population Growth.* Cambridge: Cambridge University Press.

Flores, D. 2001. *The Natural West: Environmental History in the Great Plains and Rocky Mountains.* Norman: University of Oklahoma Press.

Forrest, S. C., H. Strand, W. H. Haskins, C. Freese, J. Proctor, and E. Dinerstein. 2004. *Ocean of Grass: A Conservation Assessment for the Northern Great Plains.* Bozeman, MT: Northern Plains Conservation Network and Northern Great Plains Ecoregion of the World Wildlife Fund. www.worldwildlife.org/what/wherewework/ngp/item1410.html.

Foss, P. O. 1960. *Politics and Grass: The Administration of Grazing on the Public Domain.* Seattle: University of Washington Press.

Freese, C. H. 1998. *Wild Species as Commodities: Managing Markets and Ecosystems for Sustainability.* Washington, DC: Island Press.

Freidel, F. 1990. *Franklin D. Roosevelt: A Rendezvous with Destiny.* Boston: Little, Brown.

Freyfogle, E. T. 2003. *The Land We Share: Private Property and the Common Good.* Washington DC: Island Press.

Henwood, William D. 1998. Grassland Protected Areas. *International Union for Conservation of Nature* 8, no. 3 (October), http://cmsdata.iucn .org/downloads/parks.oct98.pdf.

H. L. Lantz Is Chosen on Appraisal Board for Fort Peck Land. 1934. *Saco Independent,* March 1, Saco, MT.

Howard, J. K. 1943. *Montana: High, Wide, and Handsome.* Lincoln: University of Nebraska Press.

Huffman, R. N.d. Untitled, unpublished manuscript. Montana State University Special Collections Library, Bozeman, MT.

Hughes, C. Max. 1988. Interview, tape recording. Montana Historical Society Archives, Helena.

Information to Go to Farmers on Land Plans. 1934. *Phillips County News,* July 26, 1A, Malta, MT.

Isenberg, A. C. 2000. *The Destruction of the Bison.* Cambridge: Cambridge University Press.

Lantz, H. L. 1935. Federal Government Land Program Stopped Here. *Phillips County News,* March 28, 1A, Malta, MT.

Lantz Is Given New Position in FSRC Setup. 1934. *Phillips County News,* May 17, 1A, Malta, MT.

Lepley, J. G. 1970. The Prince and the Artist on the Upper Missouri. *Montana: The Magazine of Western History* 20: 42–54.

Licht, D. 1997. *Ecology and Economics of the Great Plains.* Lincoln: University of Nebraska Press.

Lott, D. F. 2002. *American Bison: A Natural History.* Berkeley: University of California Press.

Lowitt, R. 1984. *The New Deal and the West.* Bloomington: Indiana University Press.

Ludlow, W. 1876. *Report of a Reconnaissance from Carroll, Montana Territory, on the Upper Missouri, to the Yellowstone Park and Return Made in the Summer of 1875.* Washington DC: Government Printing Office.

Malone, M. P., Richard B. Roeder, and William L. Lang. 1991. *Montana: A History of Two Centuries.* Seattle: University of Washington Press.

Manning, R. 1995. *Grassland: The History, Biology, Politics and Promise of the American Prairie.* New York: Viking.

———. 2004. *Against the Grain: How Agriculture Hijacked Civilization.* New York: North Point Press.

Many Dams Are Being Constructed to Conserve Water. 1936. *Saco Independent,* July 16, 1A, Saco, MT.

Martin, A. 1976. *James J. Hill and the Opening of the Northwest.* St. Paul: Minnesota Historical Society Press.

McDean, H. C. 1984. M. L. Wilson and the Origins of Federal Farm Policy in the Great Plains. 1909–1914. *Montana: The Magazine of Western History* 34: 50–59.

McDonald, V. S. 2002. "A Paper of, by, and for the People": The Producers News and the Farmers' Movement in Northeastern Montana. In *Montana Legacy: Essays on History, People and Place,* ed. H. W. Fritz, M. Murphy, and R. R. Swartout Jr., 152–76. Helena: Montana Historical Society Press.

Miller, G. 1940. History of the Livestock Industry in Phillips County.

Unpublished manuscript from the Federal Writers' Project. Montana State University, Bozeman, WPA Collection.

Milner, C. A. 1987. The Shared Memory of Montana Pioneers. *Montana: The Magazine of Western History* 37: 2–13.

Montana Land Use Planning Section. 1938. Three-Quarters of a Century's Philosophy, Opinion, and Research on Agricultural Problems in the Great Plains. Typescript. Division of Land Utilization, Farm Security Administration, USDA. Montana State University, Merrill G. Burlingame Special Collections, Bozeman, MT.

Morgan, T. 1985. *FDR: A Biography.* New York: Simon and Schuster.

Morris, E. 1979. *The Rise of Theodore Roosevelt.* New York: Ballantine Books.

———. 2001. *Theodore Rex.* New York: Modern Library.

A Move to Care for 25,000 People in Saco Valley. 1934. *Saco Independent,* February 14, Saco, MT.

Murphy, M. 2003. *Hope in Hard Times: New Deal Photographs of Montana, 1936–1942.* Helena: Montana Historical Society Press.

Nixon, E. B. 1957. *Franklin D. Roosevelt and Conservation 1911–1945.* Hyde Park, NY: General Services Administration, National Archives and Records Service, Franklin D. Roosevelt Library.

One Hundred Fifty Live in Tent Town. 1934. *Phillips County News,* June 14, 1A, Malta, MT.

Pearlstein, S. 2005. Red States Make a Mockery of Self-Reliance. *Washington Post,* January 19, E1.

Peffer, E. L. 1951. *The Closing of the Public Domain.* Stanford, CA: Stanford University Press.

Pielou, E. C. 1991. *After the Ice Age: The Return of Life of Glaciated North America.* Chicago: University of Chicago Press.

Porter, J. C. 2002. Marvelous Figures, Astonished Travelers: The Montana Expedition of Maximilian, Prince of Wied. In *Montana Legacy: Essays on History, People, and Place,* ed. H. W. Fritz, M. Murphy, and R. R. Swartout Jr., 1–26. Helena, MT: Montana Historical Society Press.

President's Visit Monday Brings Out Thousands. 1934. *Saco Independent,* August 9, 1A, Saco, MT.

Resettlement Administration. 1937. Sponsored talks. KOA Radio Station, Denver, April 18.

Rivenes, David. 1988. Interview, tape recording. Montana Historical Society Archives, Billings.

Saindon, B. 1977. Fort Peck Dam: Taming the Missouri and Treating the Depression. *Montana: The Magazine of Western History* 27: 34–55.

Sandoz, M. 1954. *The Buffalo Hunters.* New York: Hastings House.

———. 1958. *The Cattlemen.* New York: Hastings House.

Saunderson, M. H. 1984. M. L. Wilson: A Man to Remember. *Montana: The Magazine of Western History* 34: 60–63.

Schlebecker, J. T. 1963. *Cattle Raising on the Plains 1900–1961.* Lincoln: University of Nebraska Press.

Silliman, L. 1974. The Carroll Trail: Utopian Enterprise. *Montana: The Magazine of Western History* 24: 3–17.

Stegner, W. 1954. *Beyond the Hundredth Meridian.* New York: Houghton, Mifflin.

Step in Boys, the Water Is Fine in New Grazing Setup. 1936. *Saco Independent,* May 4, 1A, Saco, MT.

Stockmen Approve New Grazing Area within Three County Limits. 1934. *Phillips County News,* May 4, 1A, Malta, MT.

Stuart, G. 1977. *Pioneering in Montana: The Making of a State, 1864–1887.* Edited by Paul C. Phillips. Lincoln: University of Nebraska Press; originally published 1925.

Toole, K. R. 1959. *Montana: An Uncommon Land.* Norman: University of Oklahoma Press.

———. 1972. *Twentieth Century Montana: A State of Extremes.* Norman: University of Oklahoma Press.

U.S. Fish and Wildlife Service. 1963. *Proposed Charles M. Russell National Wildlife Range.* Washington DC: U.S. Department of the Interior. Unpaginated.

———. 1984. *The CMR Grazing Controversy: A Brief History.* Washington DC: U.S. Department of the Interior, August.

Watkins, T. H. 1990. *Righteous Pilgrim: The Life and Times of Harold L. Ickes 1874–1952.* New York: Henry Holt.

Webb, W. P. 1931. *The Great Plains.* Boston: Ginn.

Wessel, T. R. 1981. Wheat for the Soviet Masses: M. L. Wilson and the Montana Connection. *Montana: The Magazine of Western History* 31: 43–53.

White, R. 1991. *It's Your Misfortune and None of My Own: A New History of the American West.* Norman: University of Oklahoma Press.

Wilson, M. L. 1951–56. The Reminiscences of Milburn Lincoln Wilson. Transcript of interviews conducted for the Oral History Research Office, Columbia University Press, New York.

Wooten, H. H. 1965. *The Land Utilization Program: 1934 to 1964.* Washington, DC: USDA Economic Research Service.

Wuerthner, G. 2002. *Welfare Ranching: The Subsidized Destruction of the American West.* Washington DC: Island Press.

INDEX

Text: 10/15 Janson

Display: Gotham

Compositor: Integrated Composition Systems

Indexer: Thérèse Shere

Cartographer: Bill Nelson

Printer/Binder: Maple-Vail Book Manufacturing Group